Spiders?

Written by

Alain M. Bergeron
Michel Quintin
Sampar

Illustrations by

Sampar

Translated by

Solange Messier

PA

First published as "Savais-tu? Les Araignées" by Éditions Michel Quintin, Québec, Canada

Published in Canada by Fitzhenry & Whiteside, 195 Allstate Parkway, Markham, Ontario L3R 4T8

Published in the United States by Fitzhenry & Whiteside, 311 Washington Street, Brighton, Massachusetts 02135

www.fitzhenry.ca godwit@fitzhenry.ca

10 9 8 7 6 5 4 3 2 1

Library and Archives Canada Cataloguing in Publication
Do You Know Spiders?
ISBN 9781554553020 (pbk.)
Data available on file

Publisher Cataloging-in-Publication Data (U.S.)
Do You Know Spiders?
ISBN 9781554553020 (pbk.)
Data available on file

Fitzhenry & Whiteside acknowledges with thanks the Canada Council for the Arts, and the Ontario Arts Council for their support of our publishing program. We acknowledge the financial support of the Government of Canada through the Canada Book Fund (CBF) for our publishing activities.

Canada Council for the Arts   Conseil des Arts du Canada

ONTARIO ARTS COUNCIL
CONSEIL DES ARTS DE L'ONTARIO
50 YEARS OF ONTARIO GOVERNMENT SUPPORT OF THE ARTS
50 ANS DE SOUTIEN DU GOUVERNEMENT DE L'ONTARIO AUX ARTS

Text and cover design by Daniel Choi
Cover image by Sampar
Printed in Canada by Friesens.

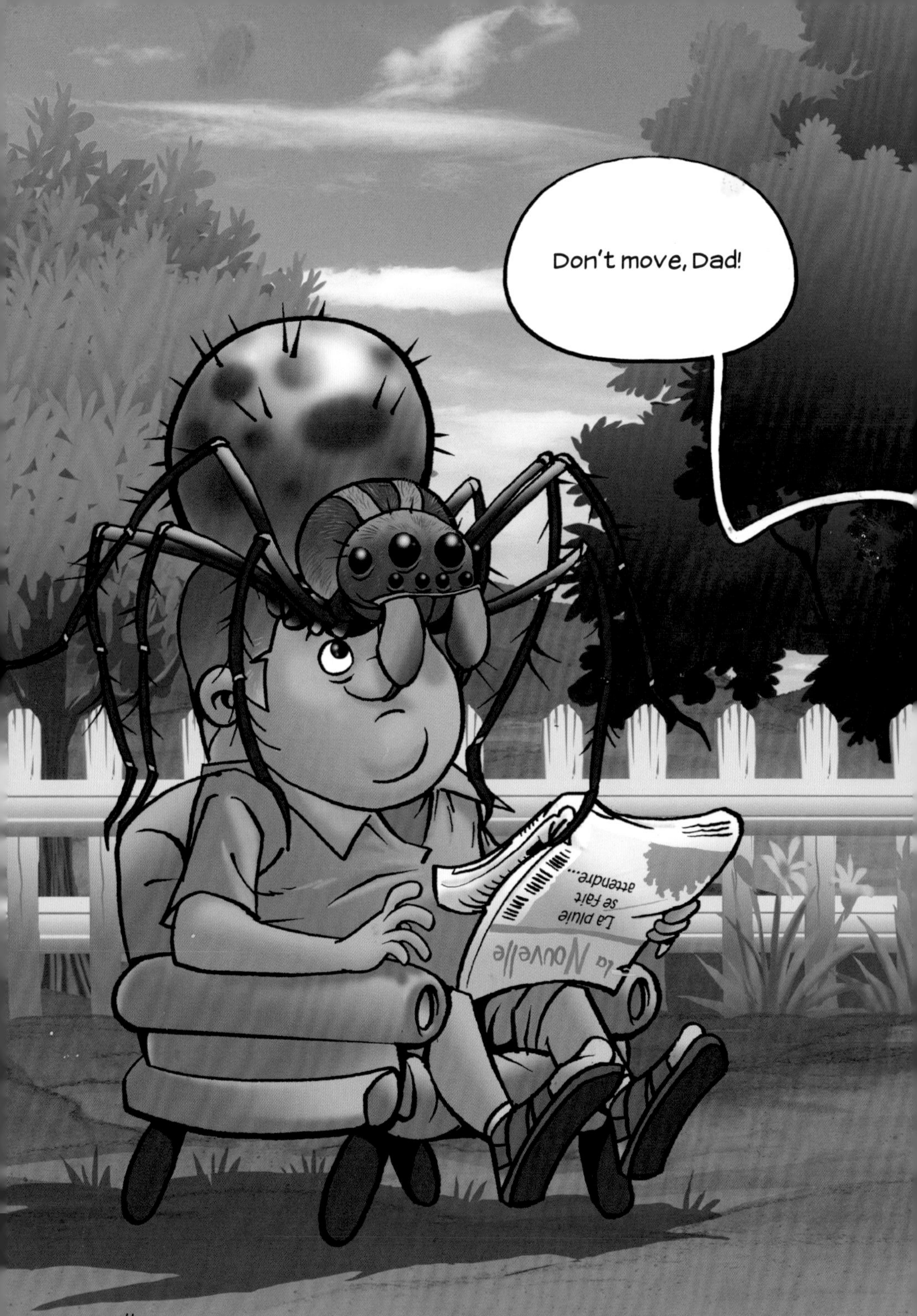
Don't move, Dad!
la Nouvelle
La pluie se fait attendre...

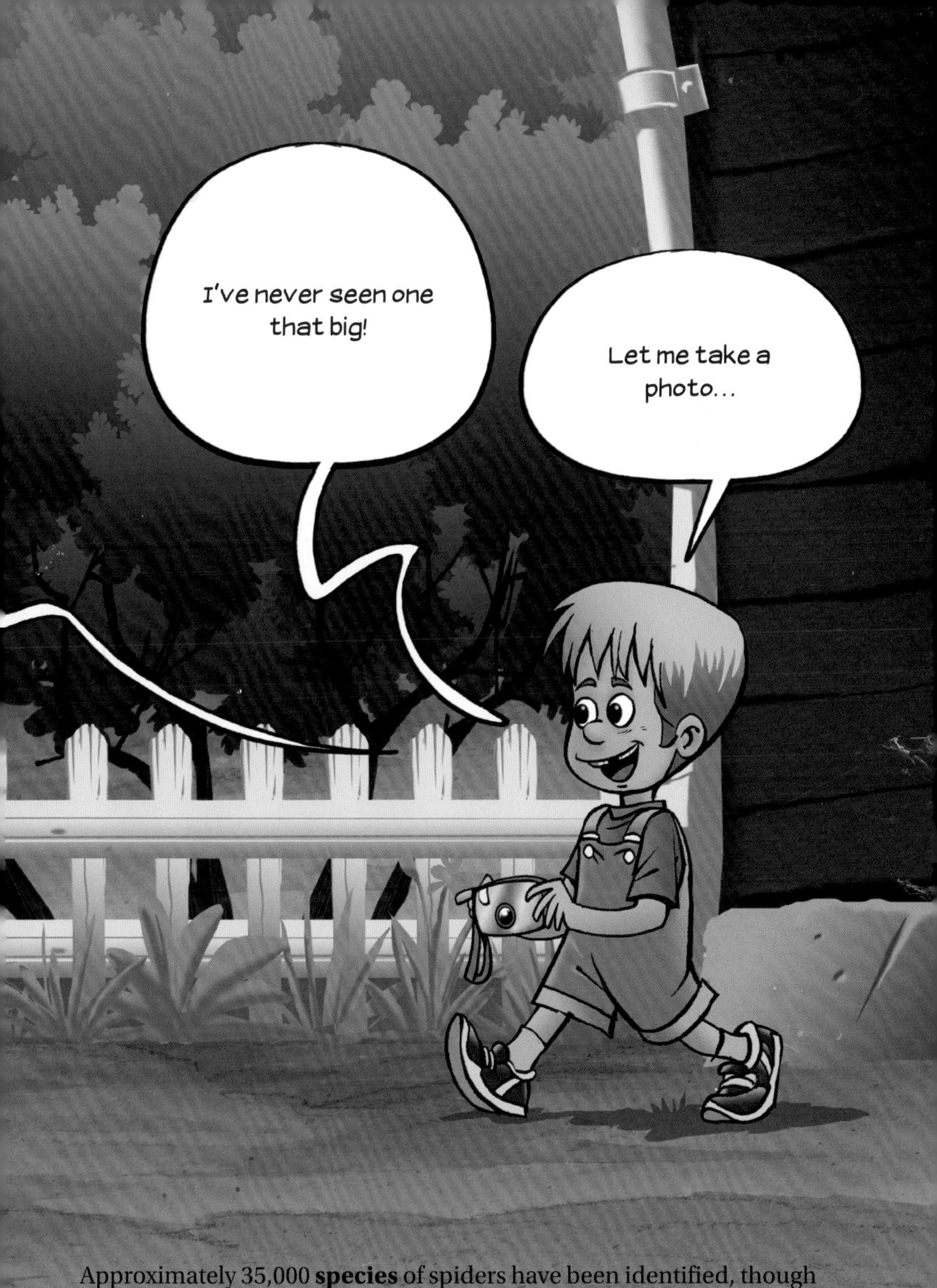
I've never seen one that big!
Let me take a photo...

Approximately 35,000 **species** of spiders have been identified, though scientists believe that thousands more have yet to be discovered.

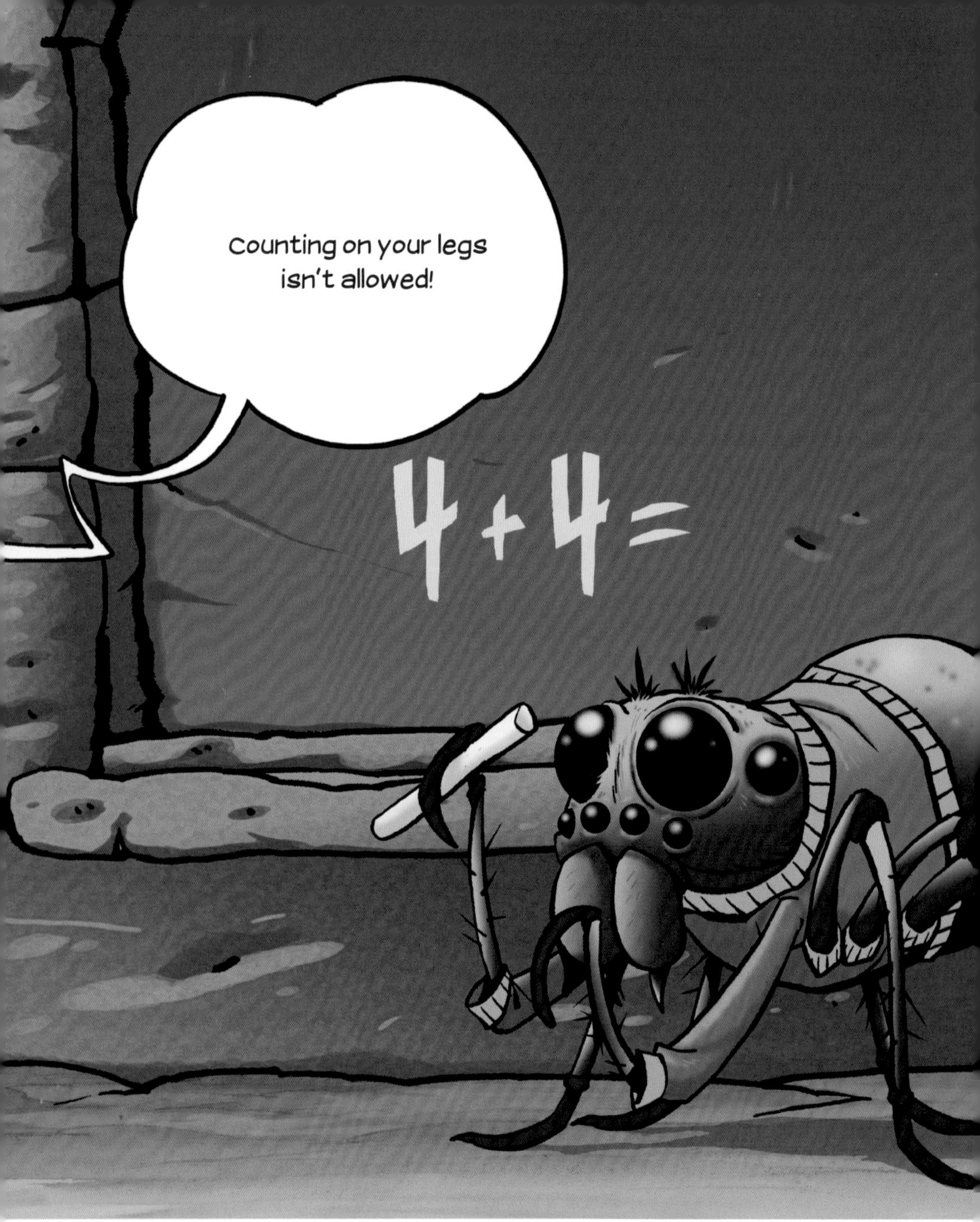
Counting on your legs isn't allowed!
4 + 4 =

These eight-legged creatures aren't actually insects; they're arachnids.

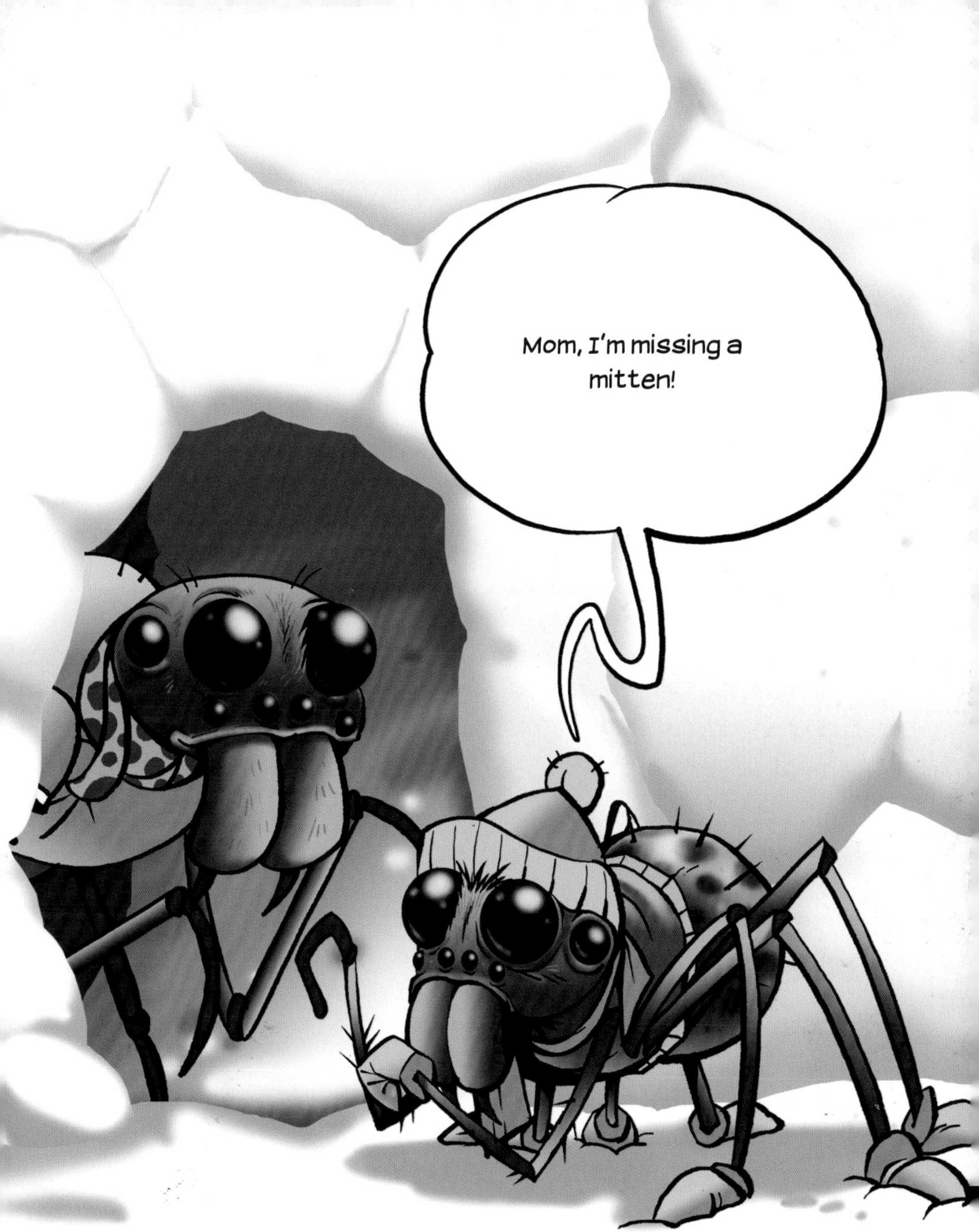
Mom, I'm missing a mitten!

Spiders can be found all around the world in every **climate** and in any environment, even in the water.

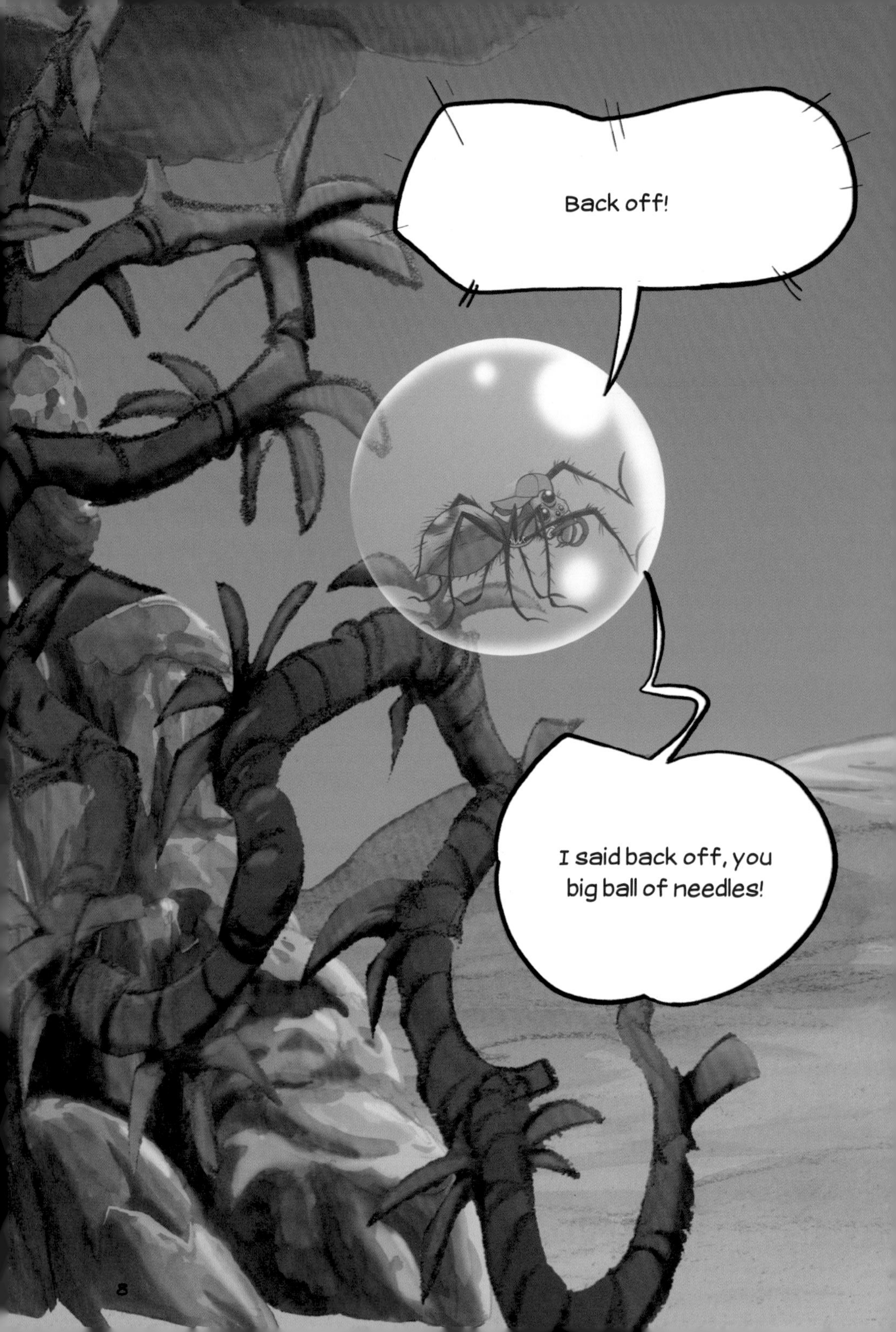
Back off!
I said back off, you big ball of needles!

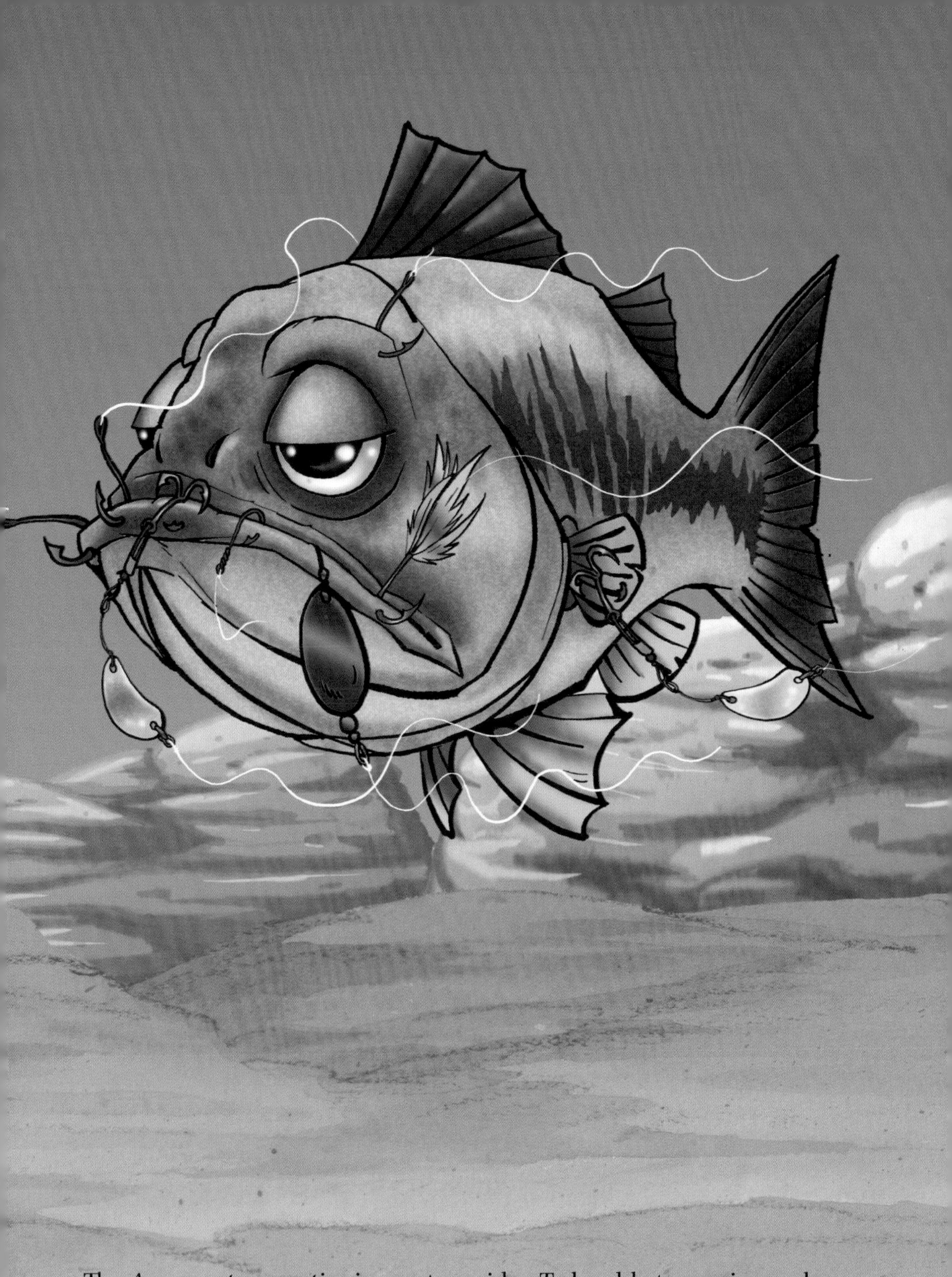

The *Argyroneta aquatica* is a water spider. To be able to survive under water, it constructs a bubble around itself and fills it with air.

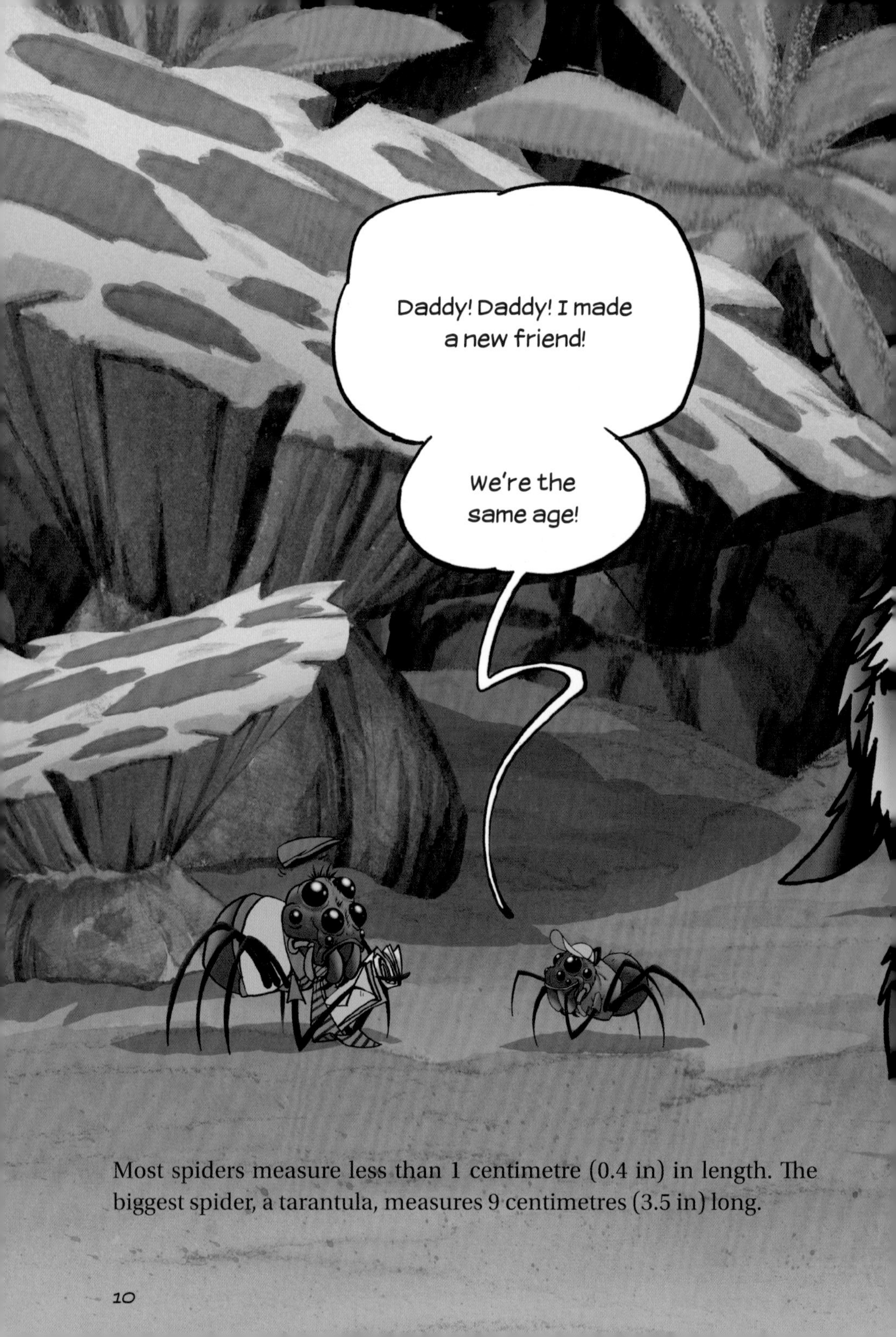
Daddy! Daddy! I made a new friend!
We're the same age!

Most spiders measure less than 1 centimetre (0.4 in) in length. The biggest spider, a tarantula, measures 9 centimetres (3.5 in) long.

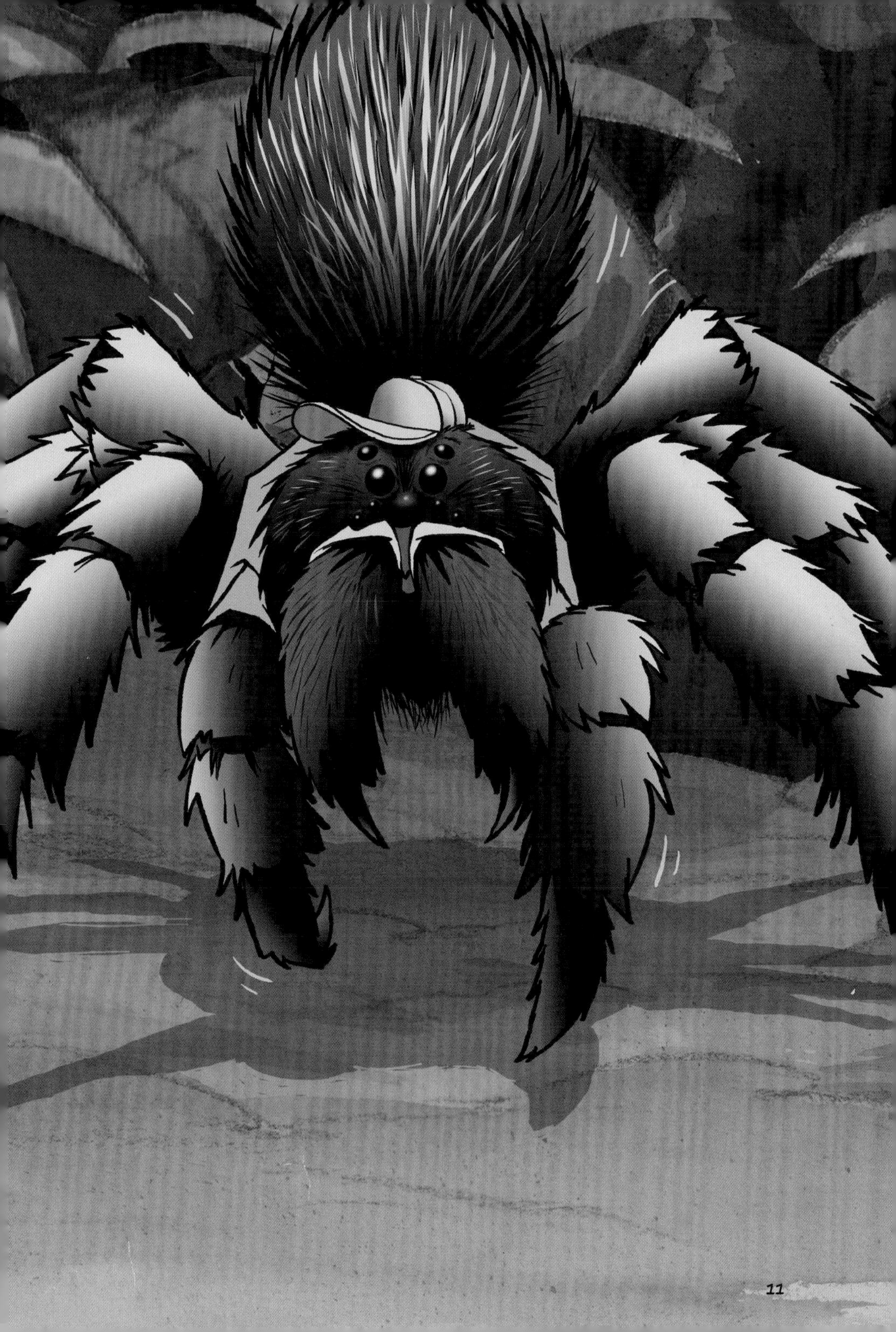

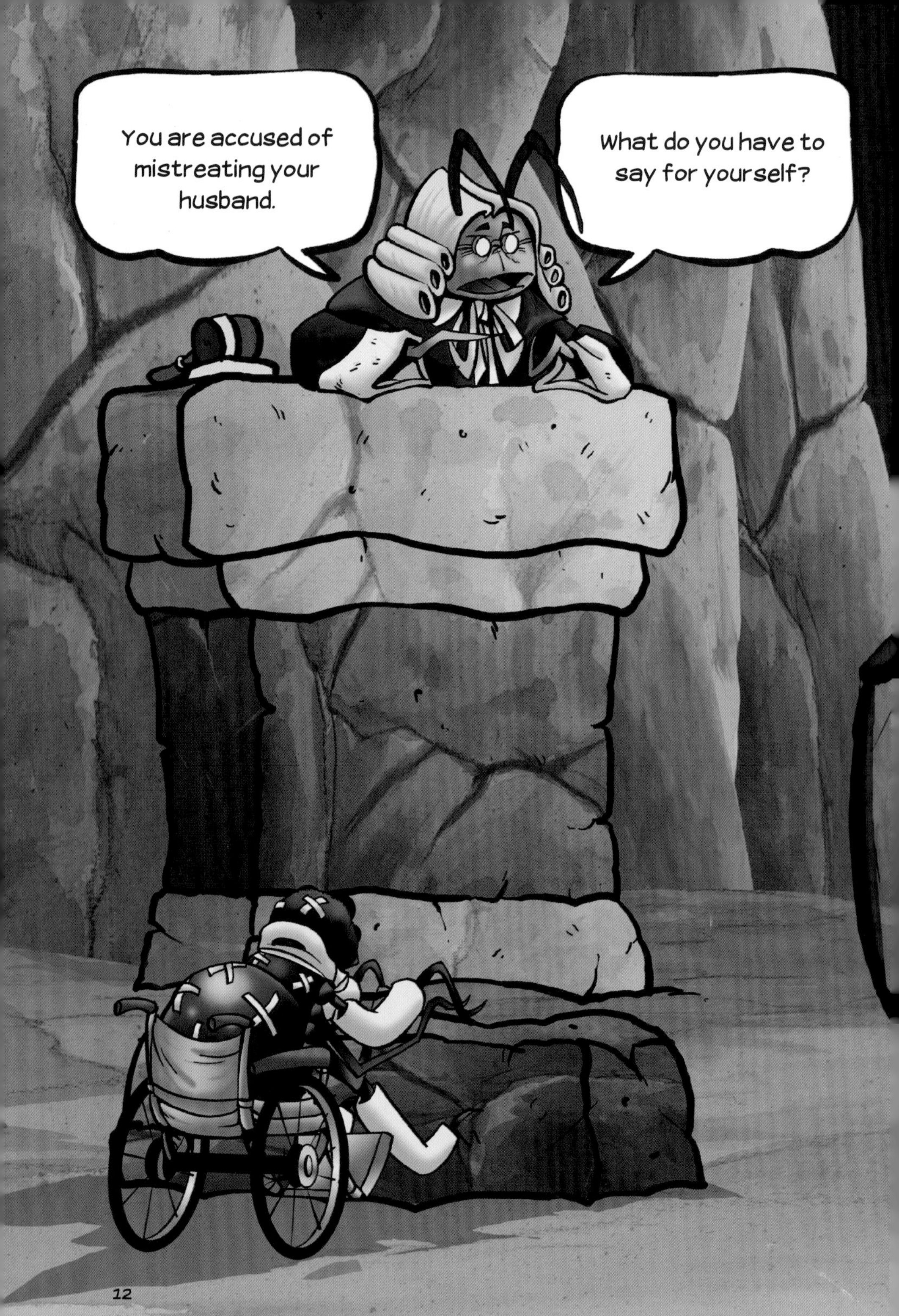
You are accused of mistreating your husband.
What do you have to say for yourself?

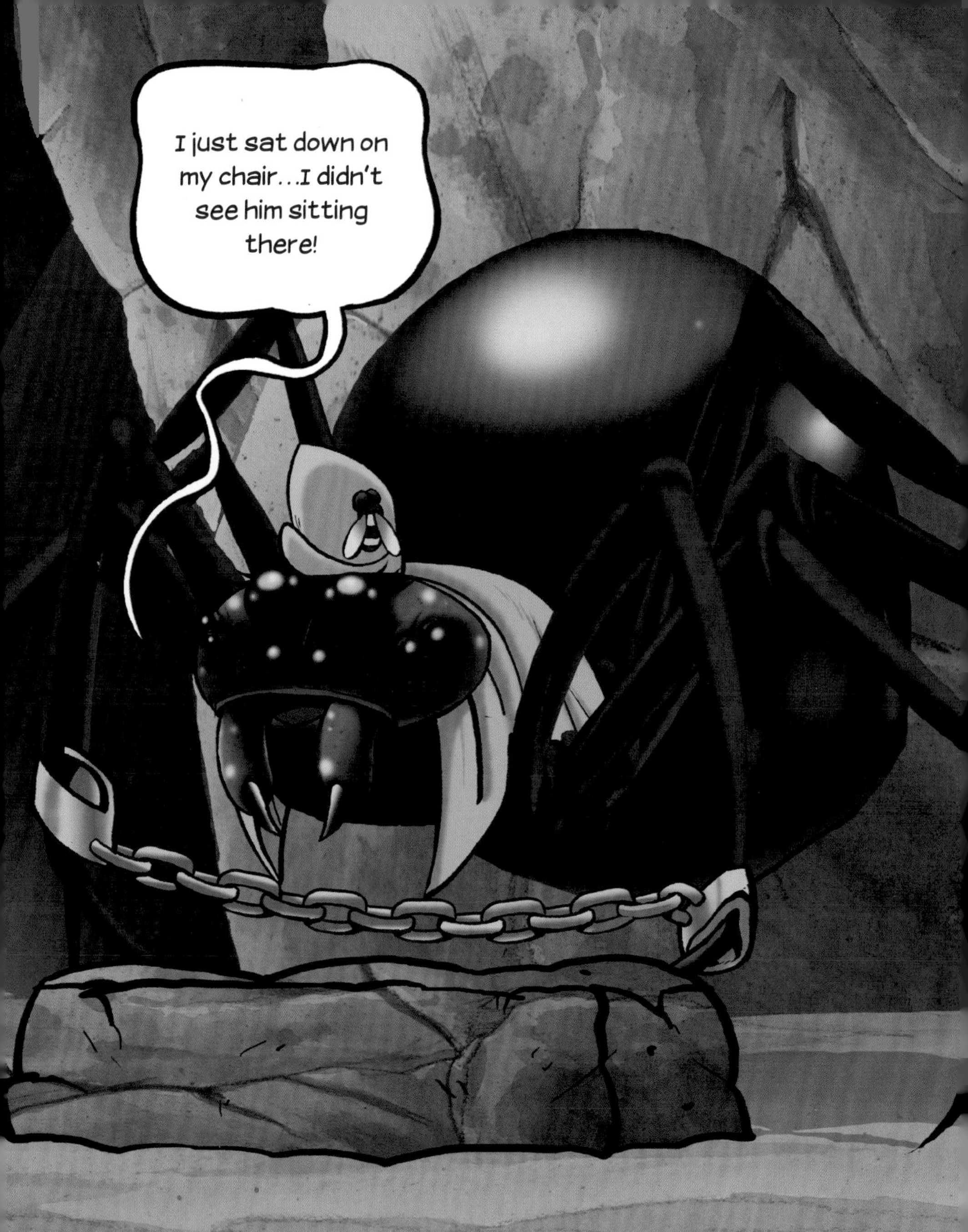
I just sat down on my chair…I didn't see him sitting there!

Within most species, the female spider is bigger and stronger than the male. Her weight can reach up to 100 times the weight of the male.

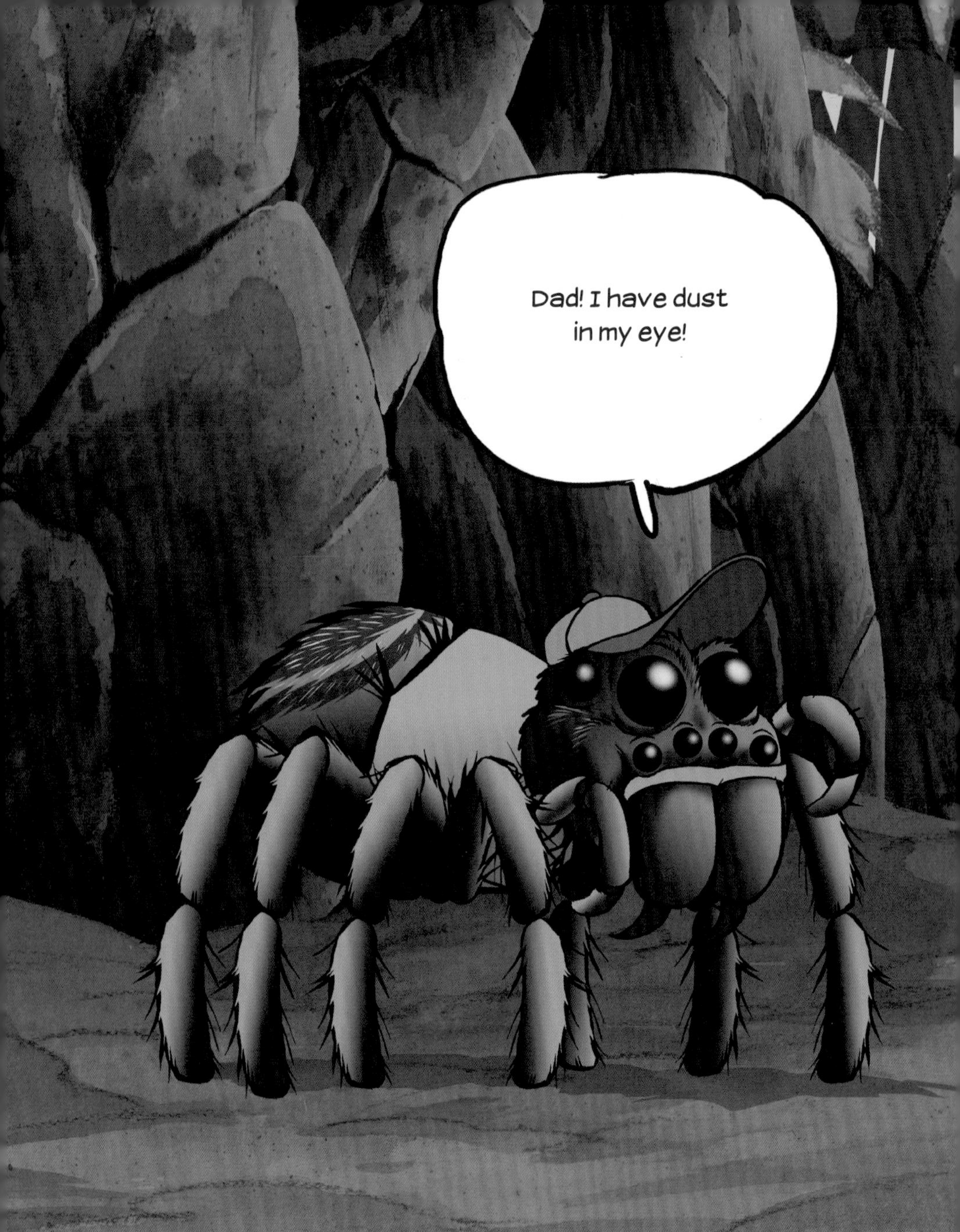
Dad! I have dust in my eye!

Even though the majority of spiders have eight eyes, some see almost nothing. They can't hear or smell anything either. Their hairs, which cover their entire bodies, replace these functions.

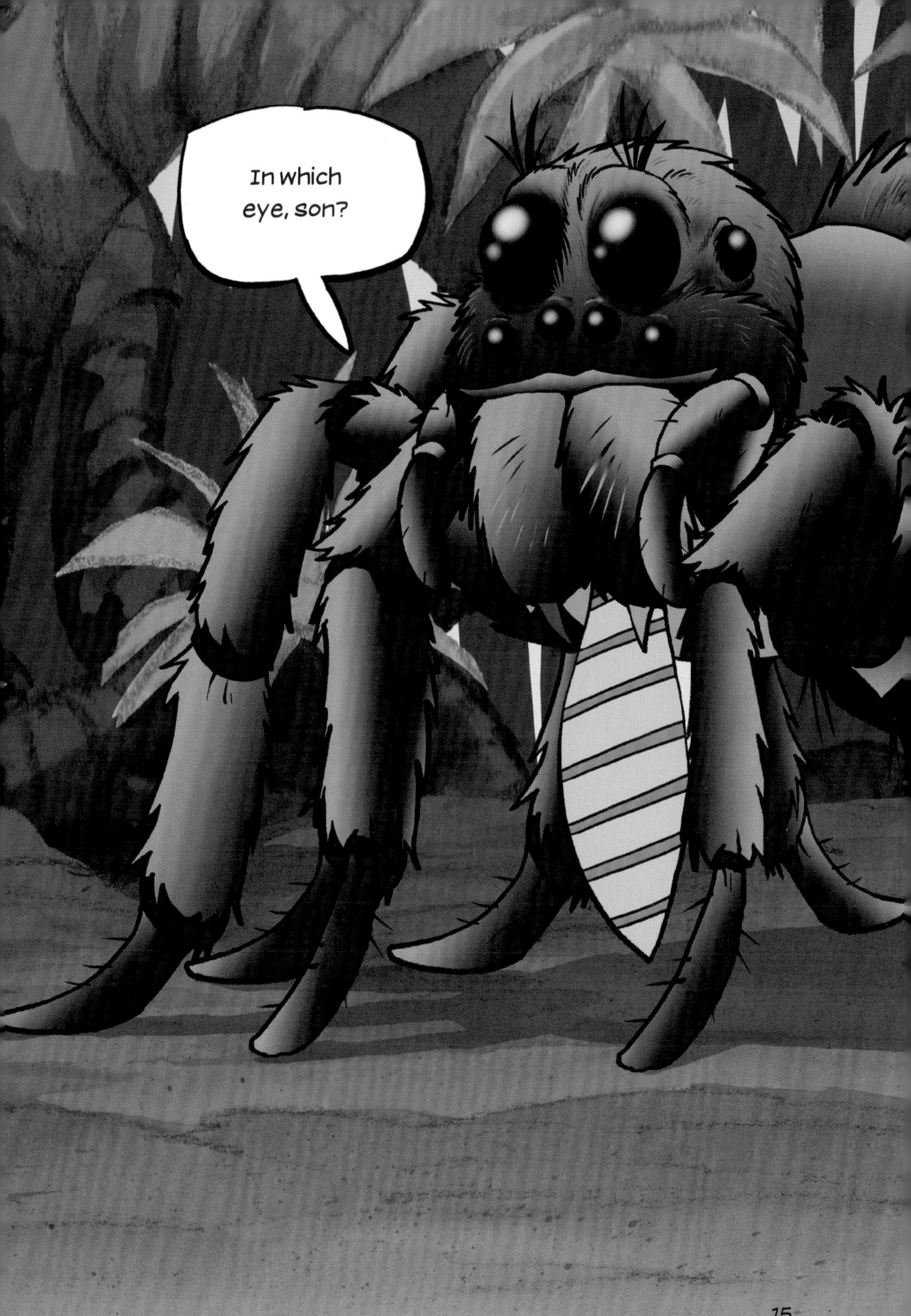
In which eye, son?

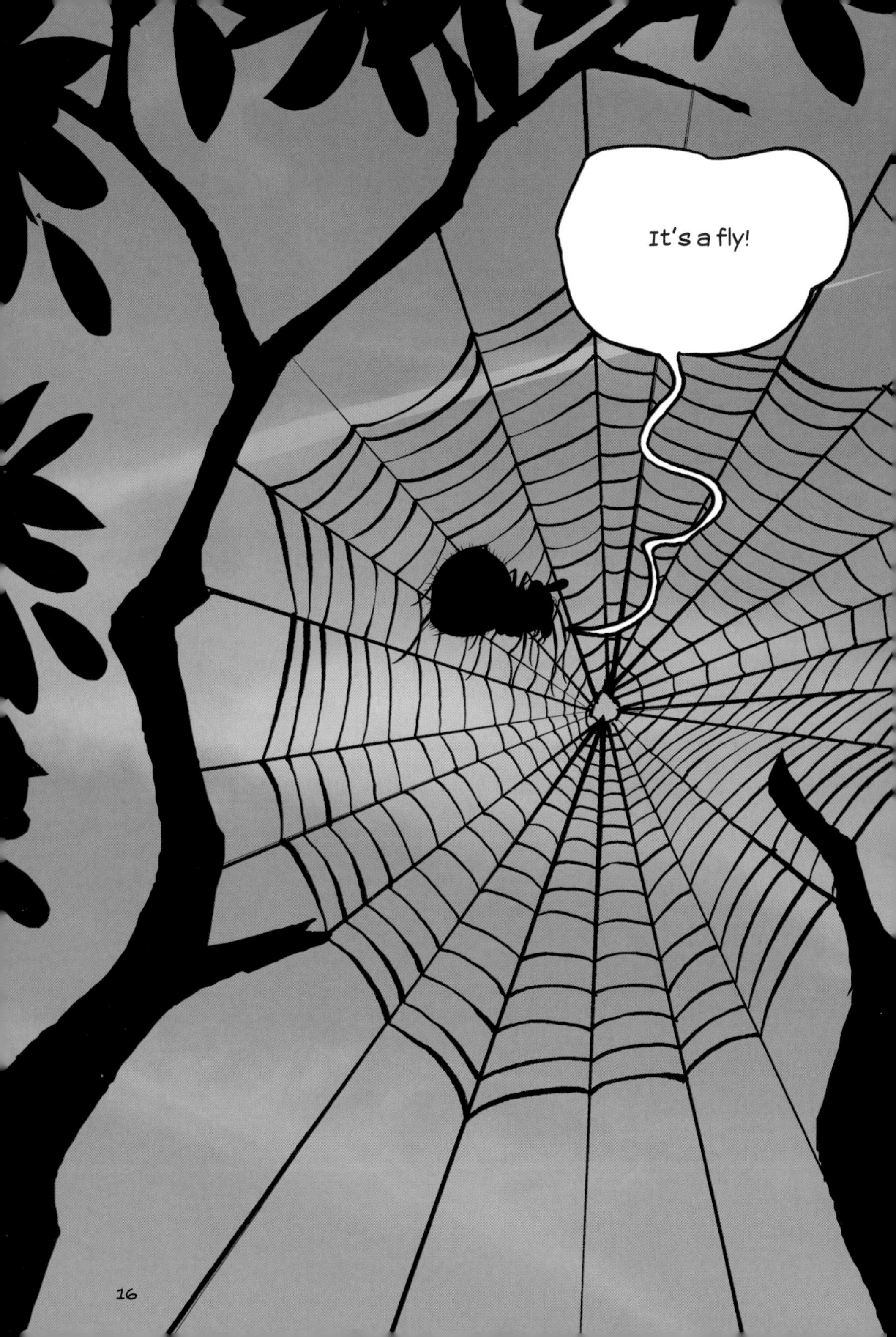
It's a fly!

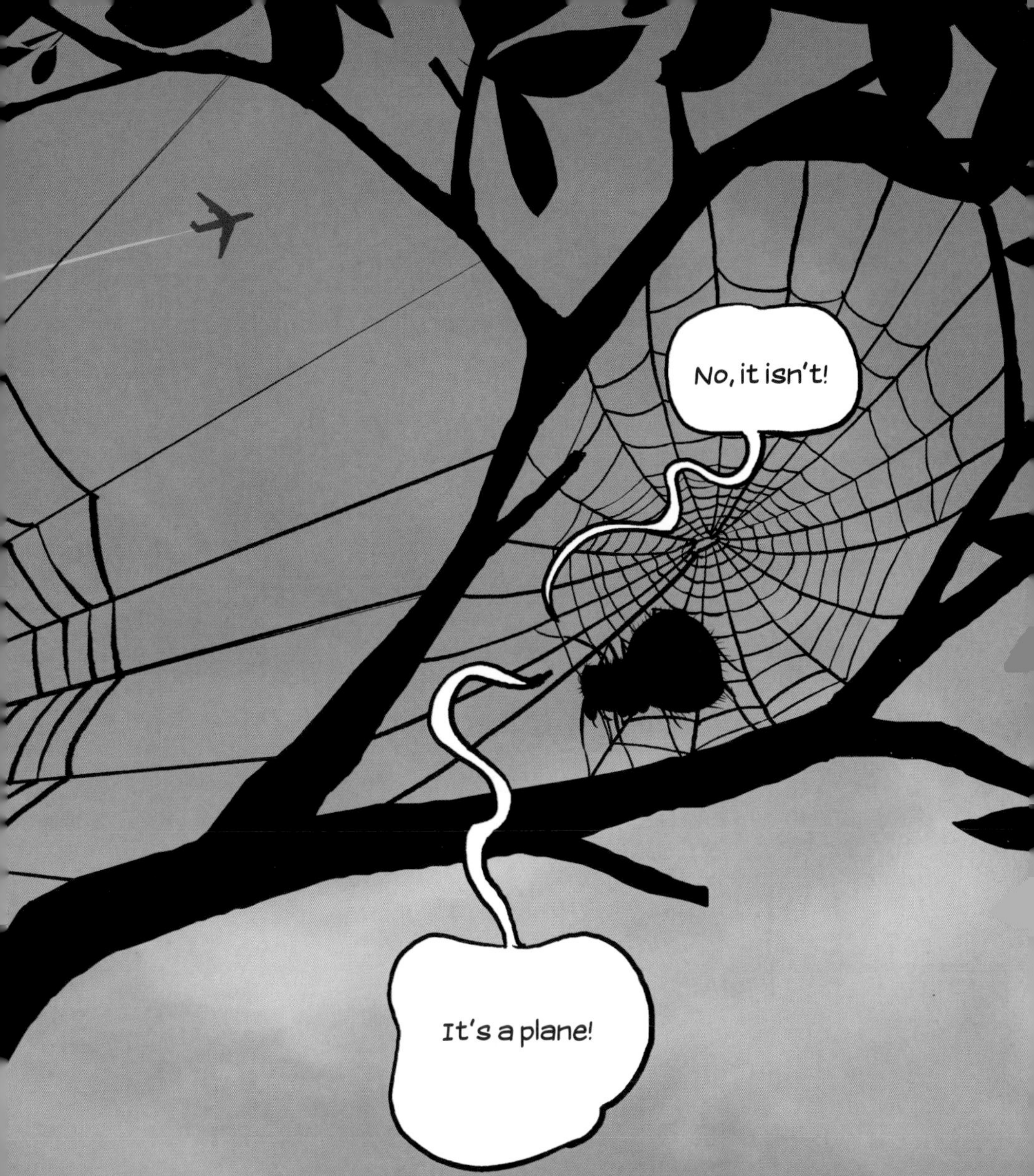
It's a plane!
No, it isn't!

Certain hairs permit the spider to detect vibrations on its web. Other hairs act like its ears. Because of these hairs, a spider can perceive vibrations in the air caused by a fly's wings flapping.

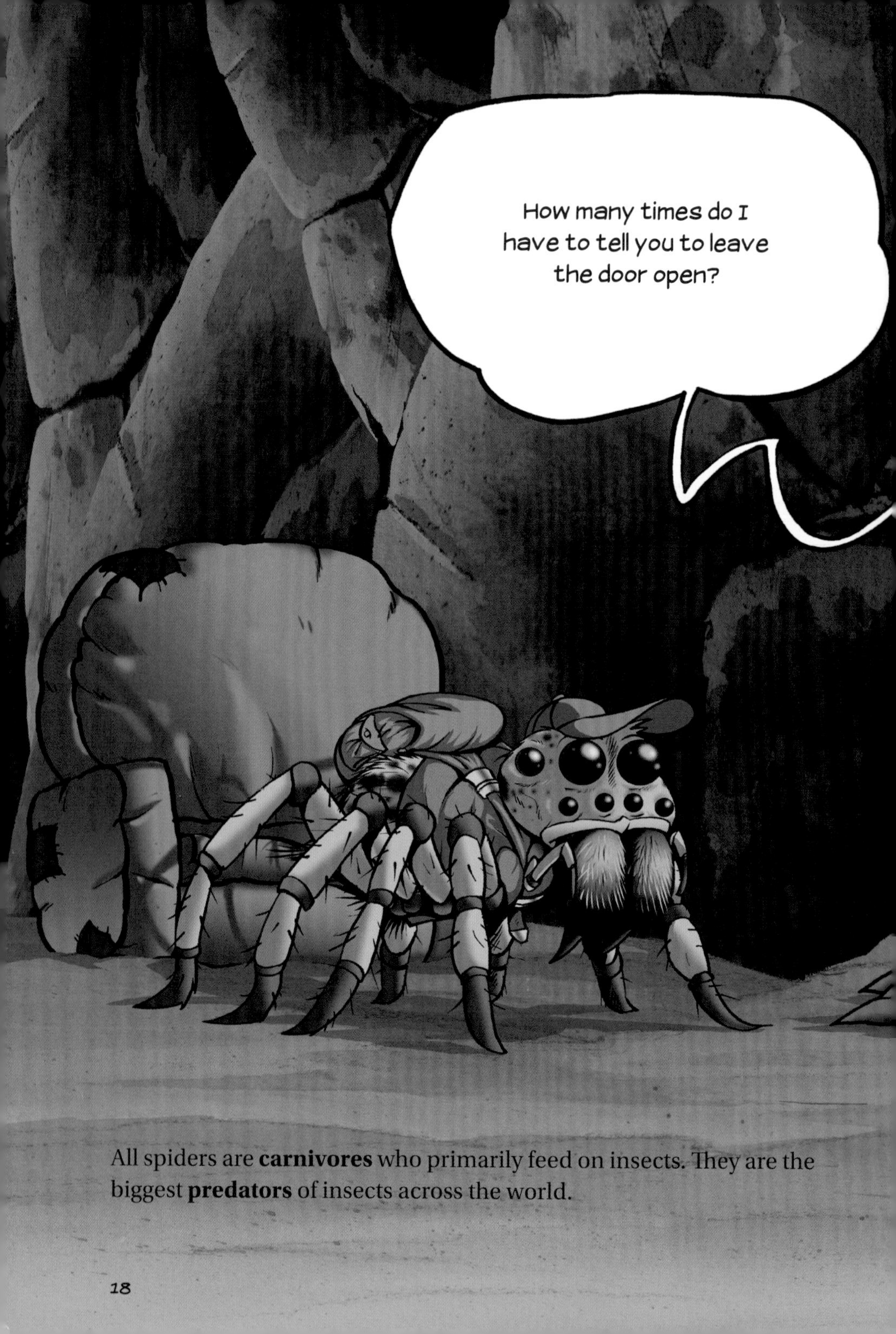
How many times do I have to tell you to leave the door open?

All spiders are **carnivores** who primarily feed on insects. They are the biggest **predators** of insects across the world.

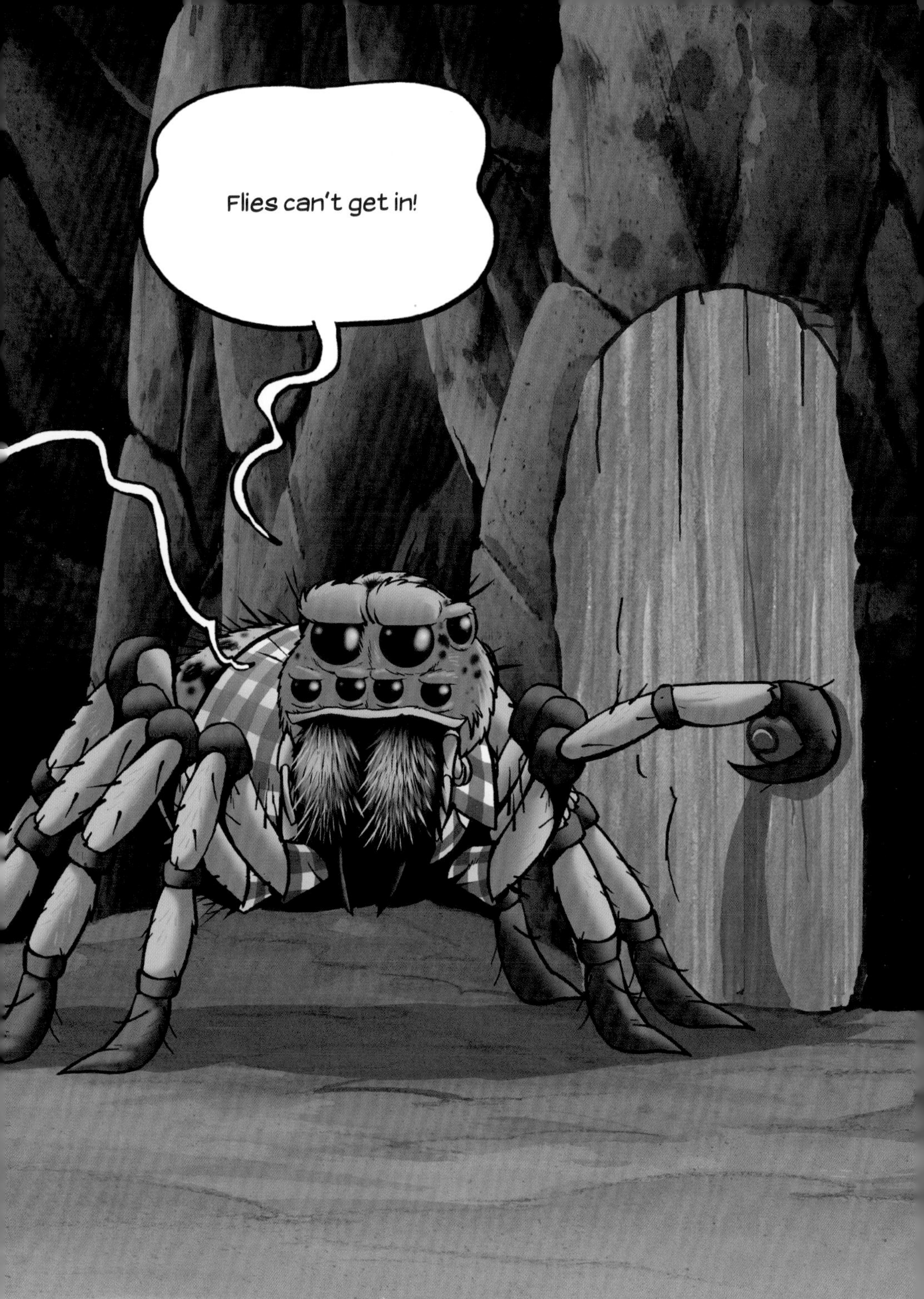
Flies can't get in!

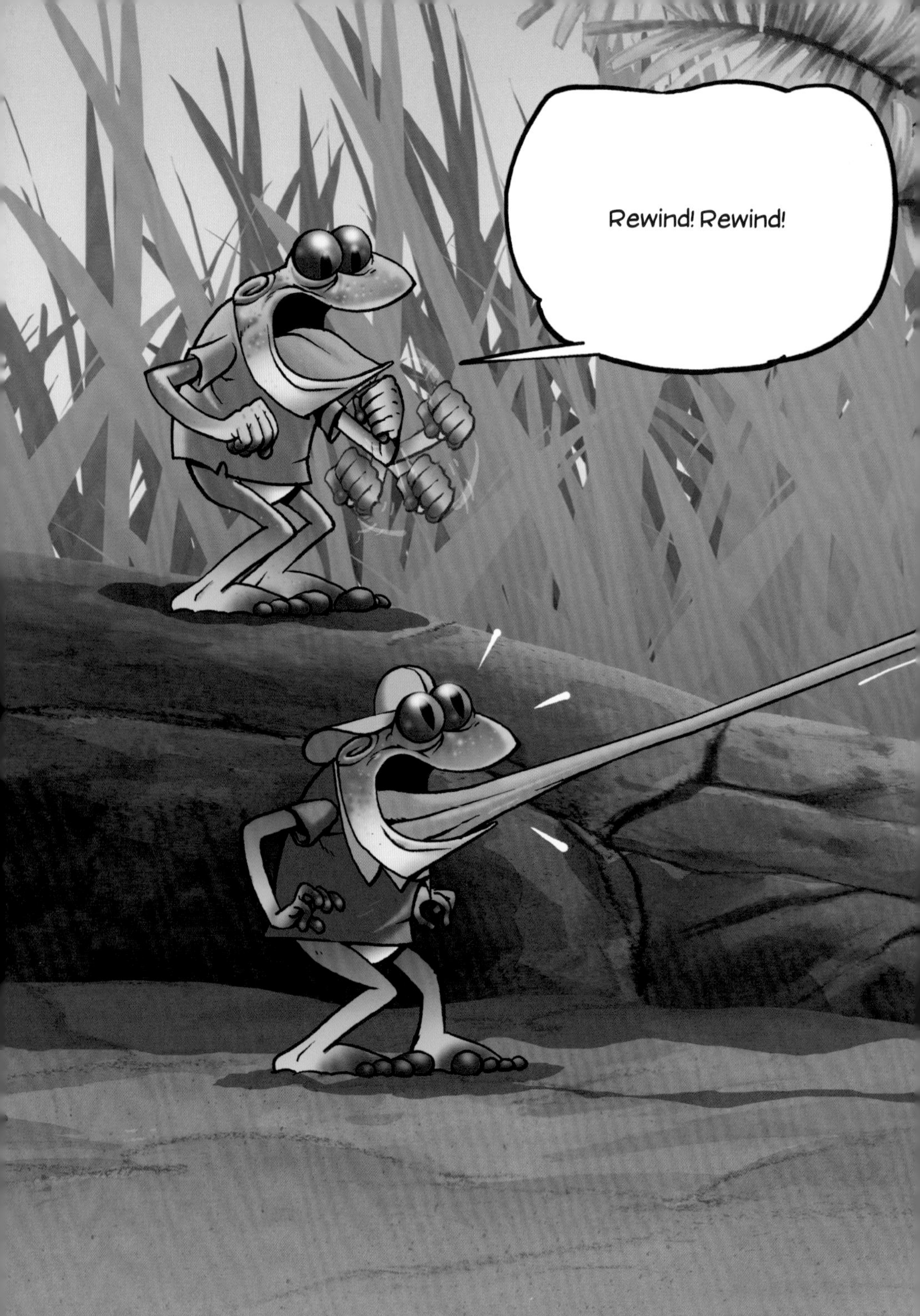
Rewind! Rewind!

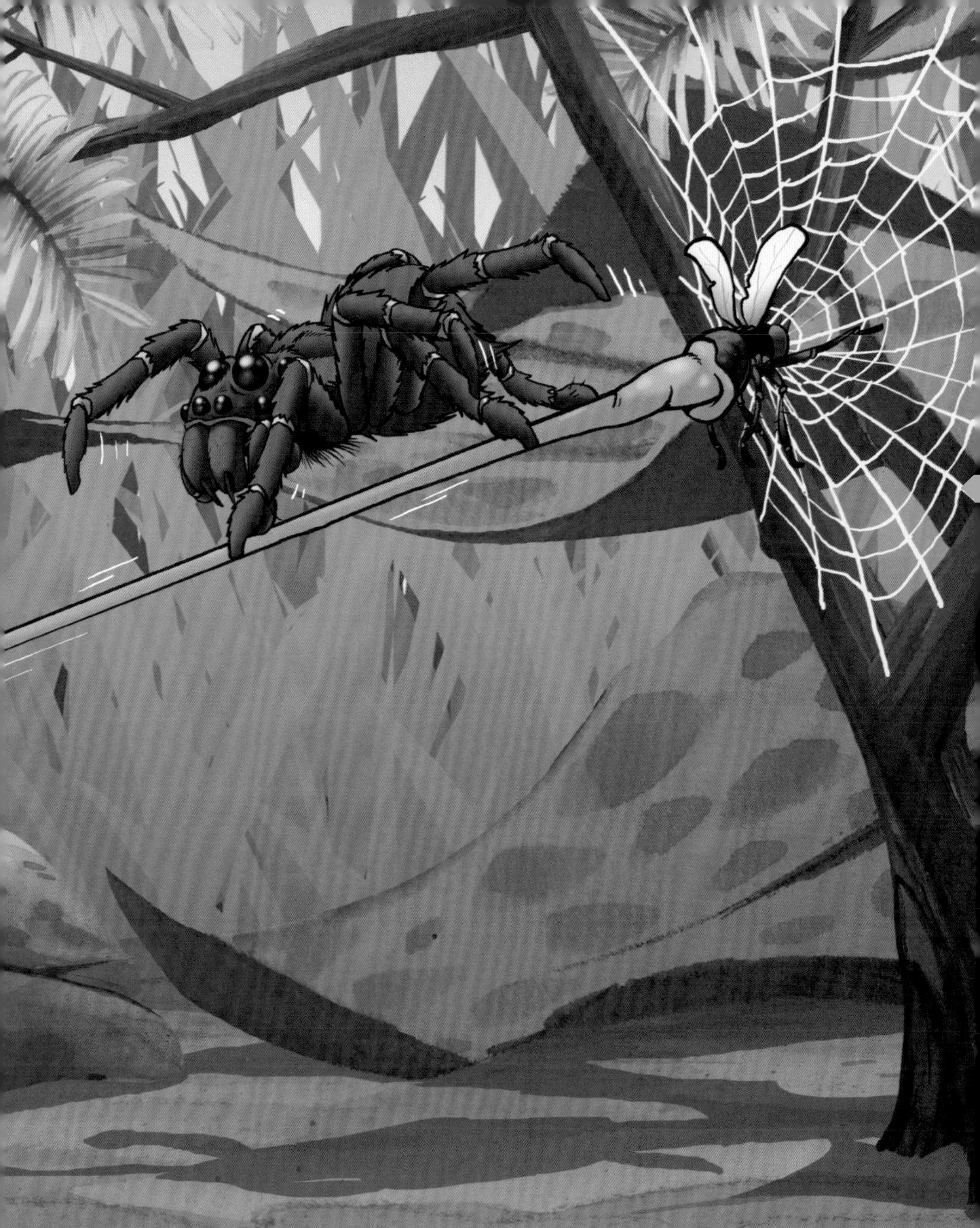

A spider's menu varies according to its species. Some species eat other spiders, **crustaceans**, small fish, frogs and even small birds.

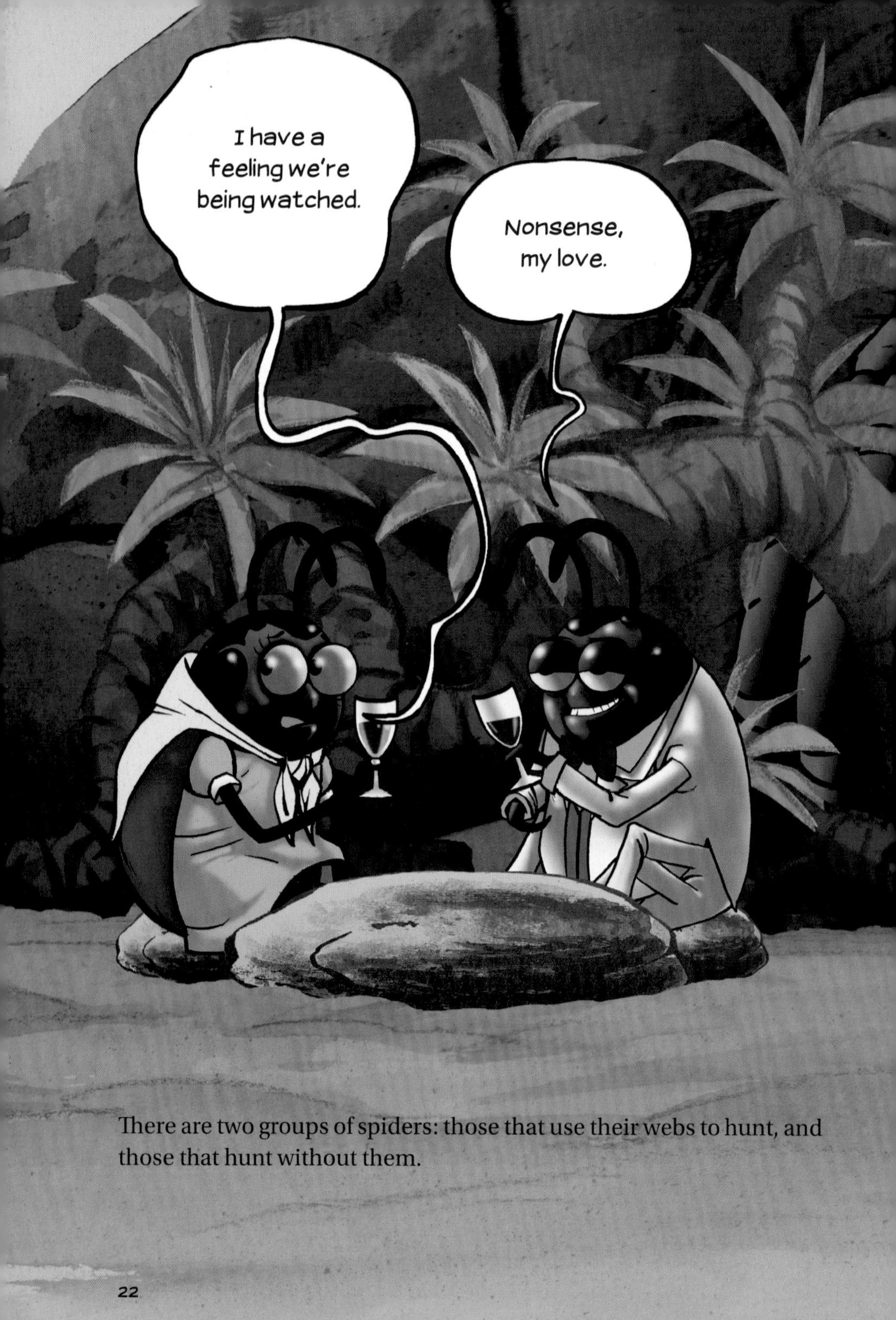
I have a feeling we're being watched.
Nonsense, my love.

There are two groups of spiders: those that use their webs to hunt, and those that hunt without them.

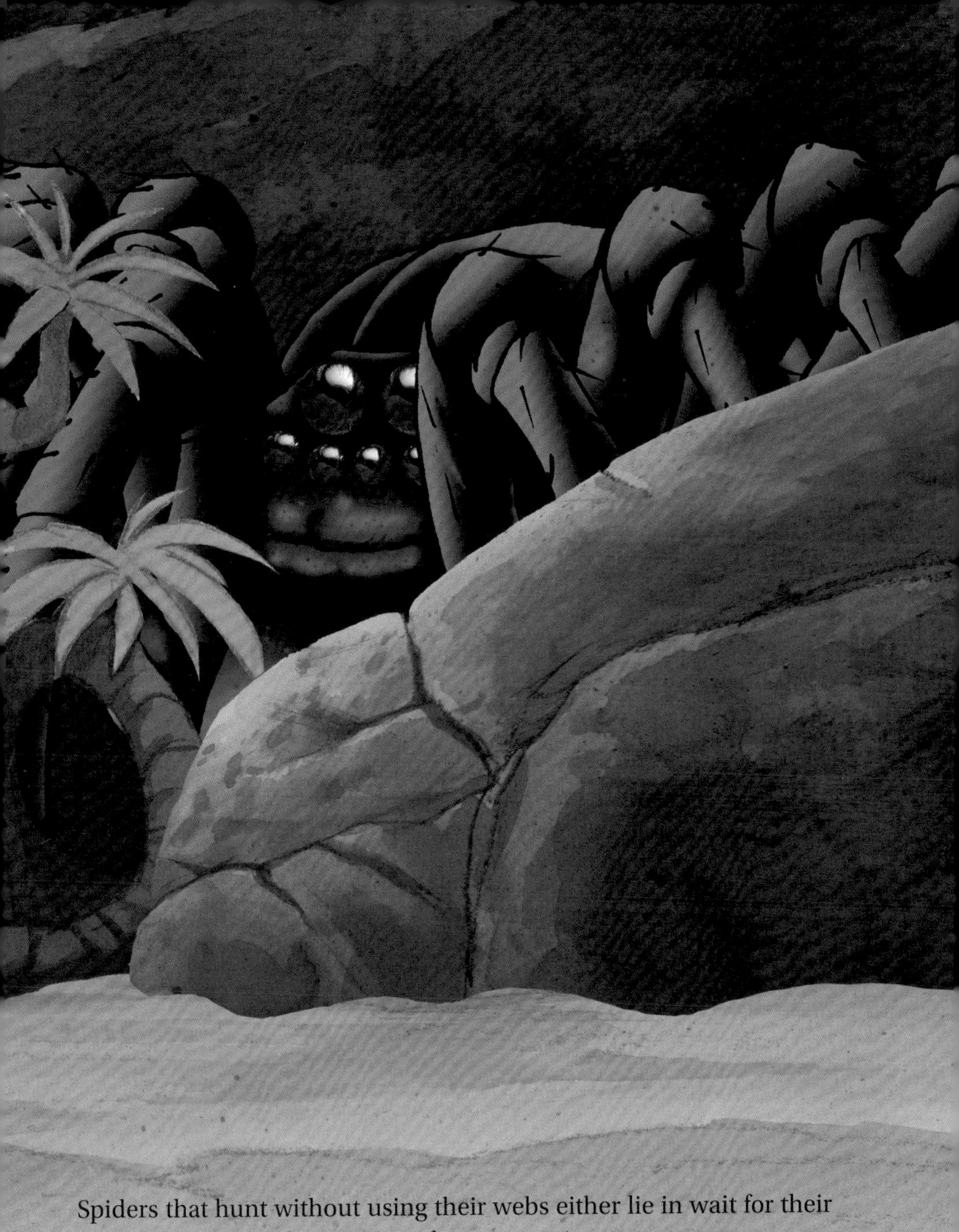

Spiders that hunt without using their webs either lie in wait for their **prey** or gently sneak up on it and pounce.

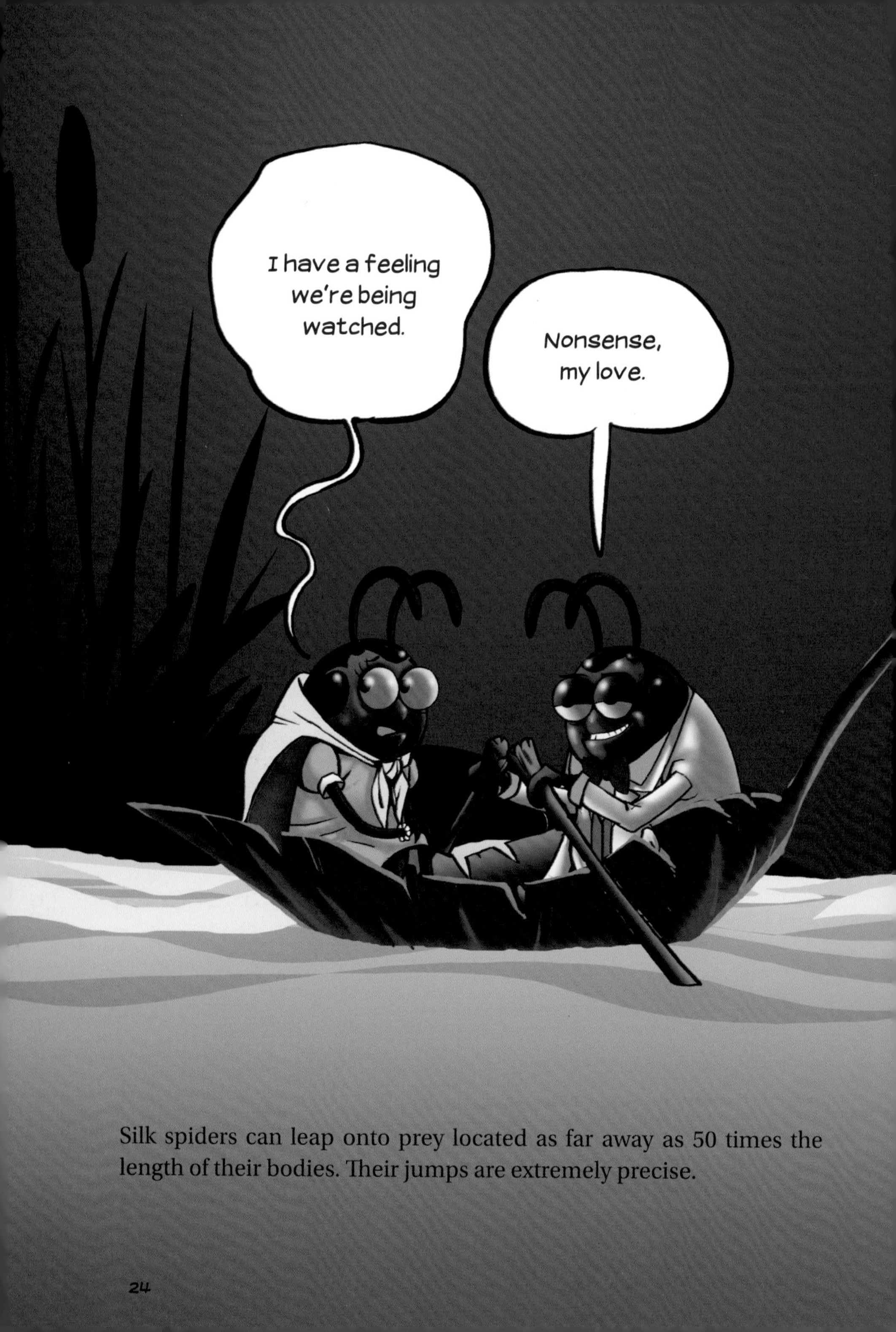
I have a feeling we're being watched.
Nonsense, my love.

Silk spiders can leap onto prey located as far away as 50 times the length of their bodies. Their jumps are extremely precise.

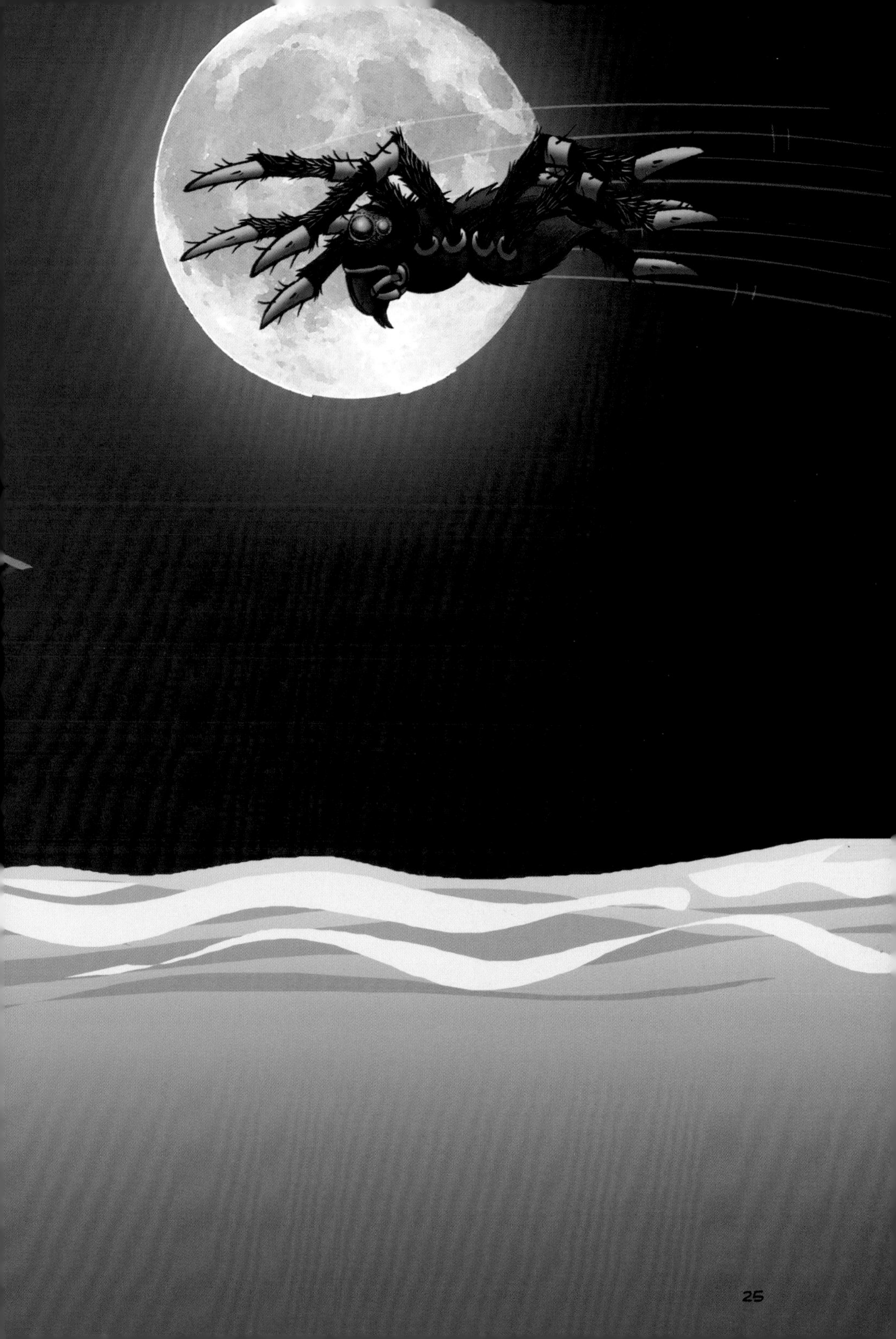

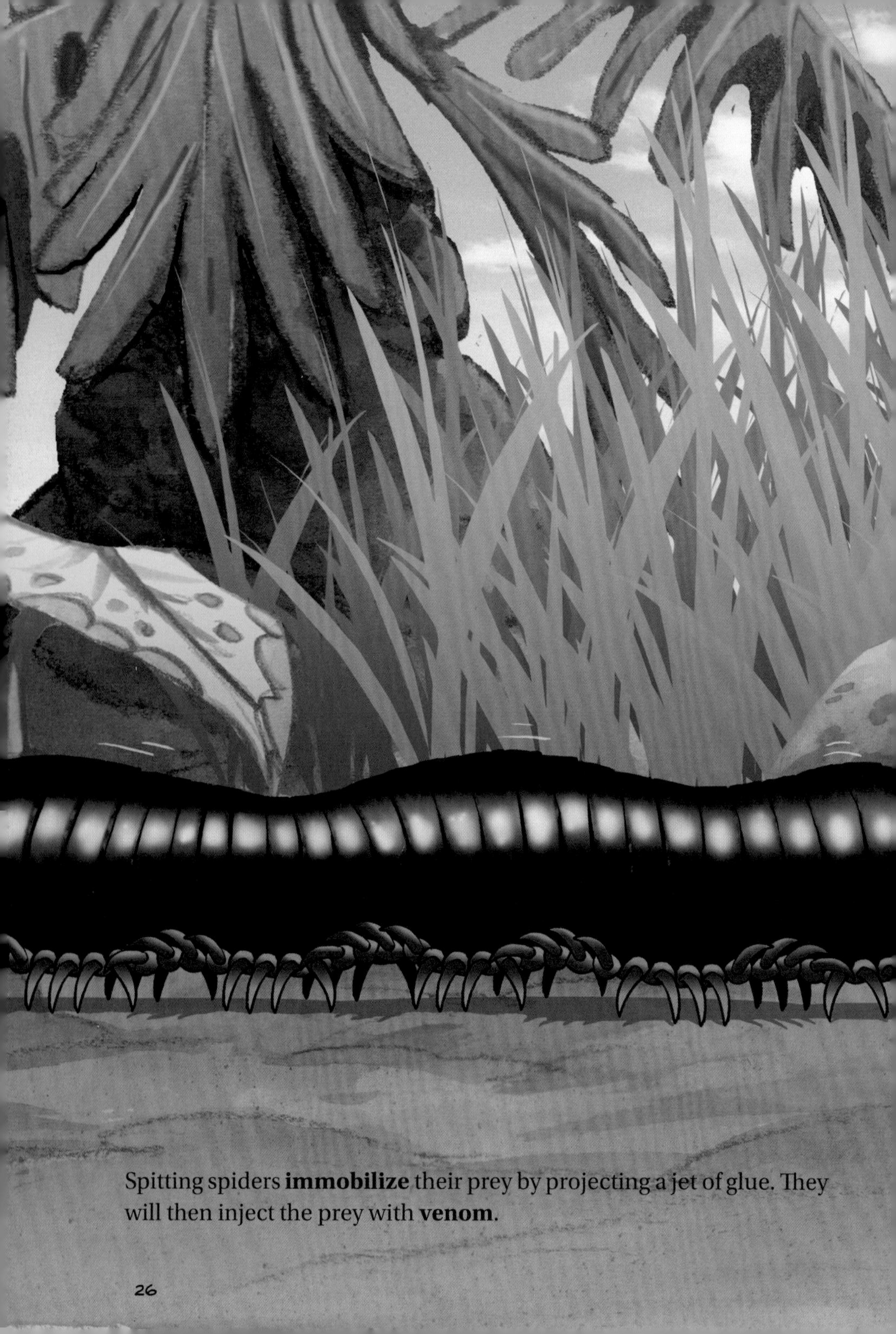

Spitting spiders **immobilize** their prey by projecting a jet of glue. They will then inject the prey with **venom**.

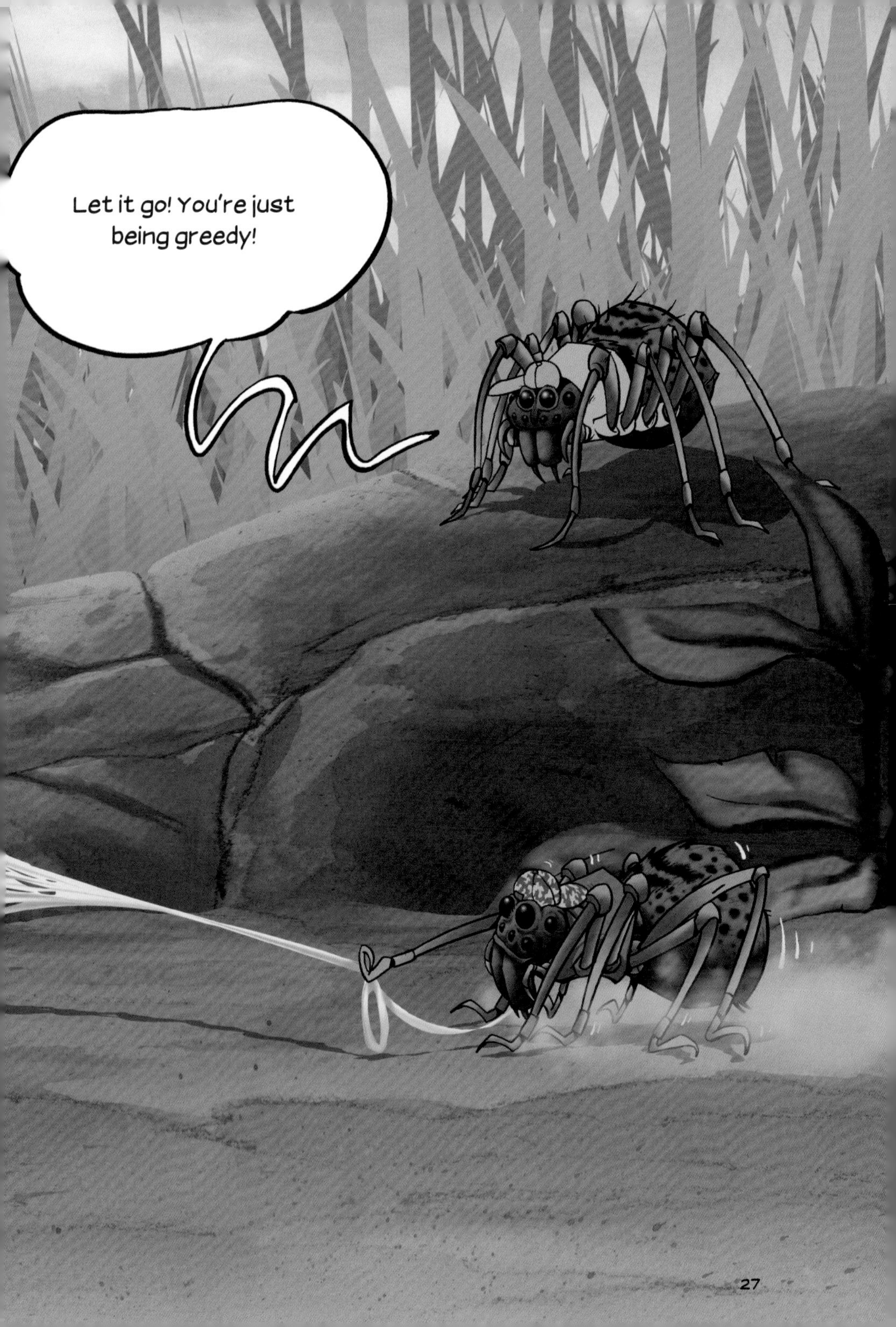
Let it go! You're just being greedy!

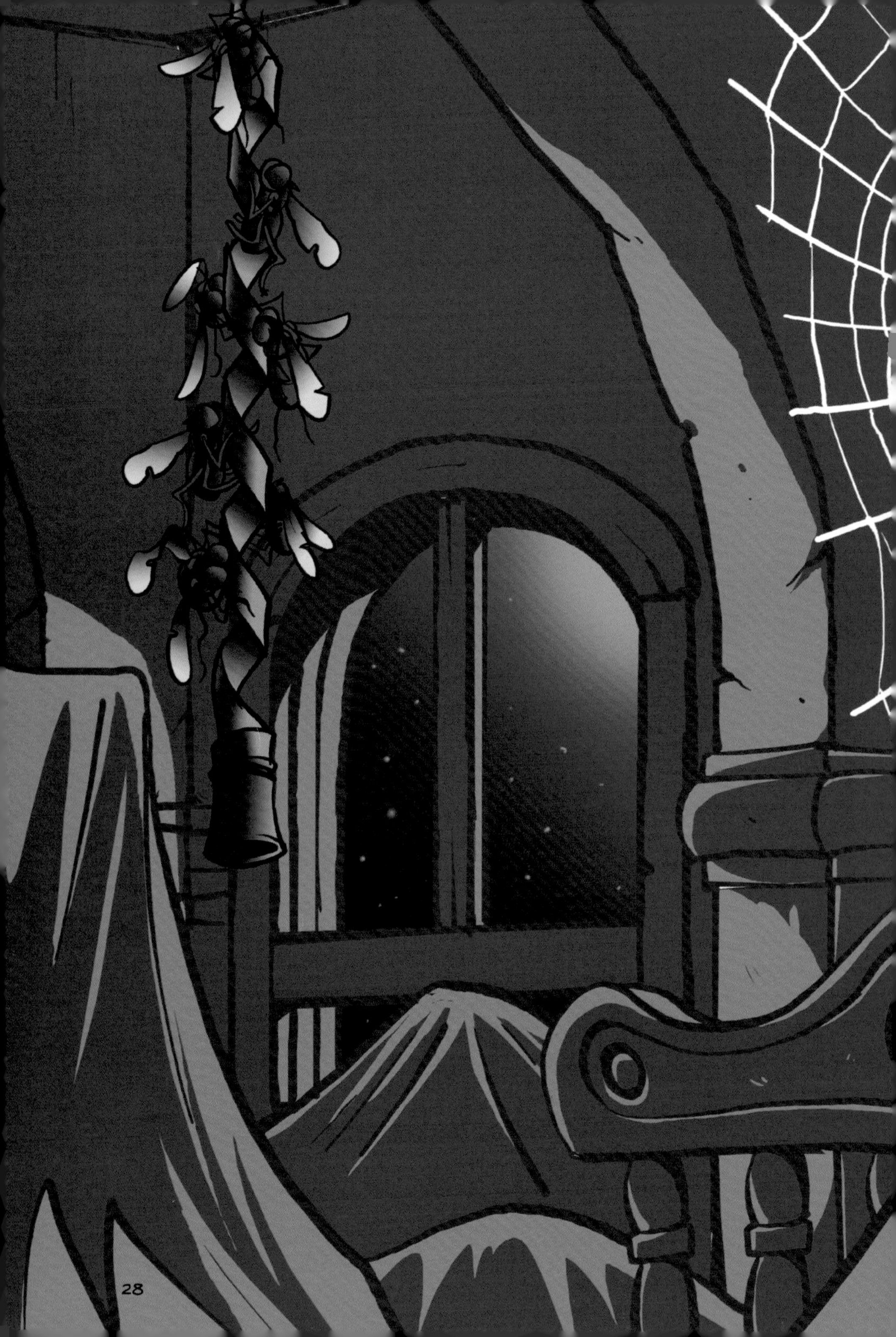

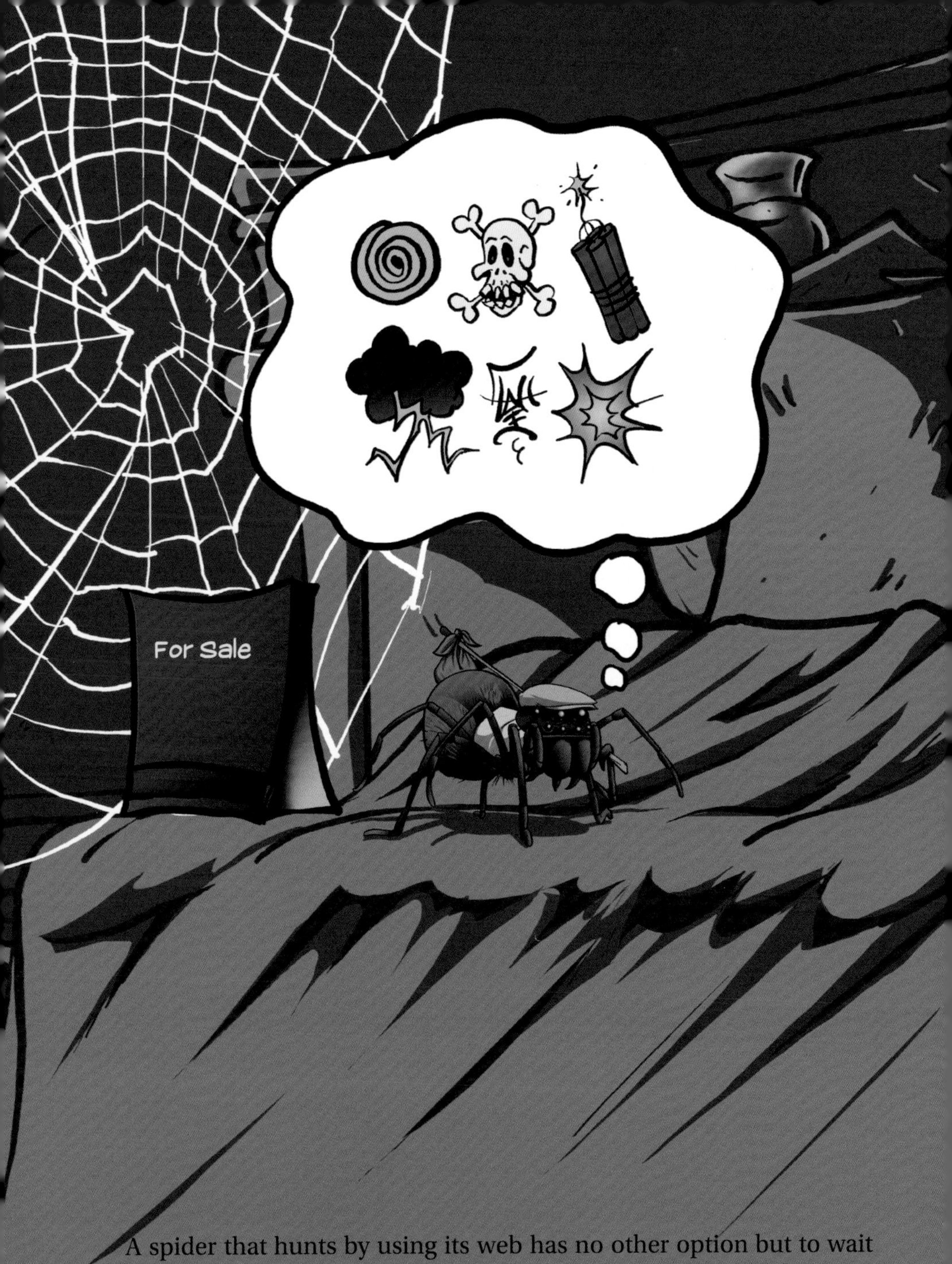
For Sale

A spider that hunts by using its web has no other option but to wait patiently for an insect to get stuck in its trap. The spider is guided to the insect by the vibrations it makes on the web.

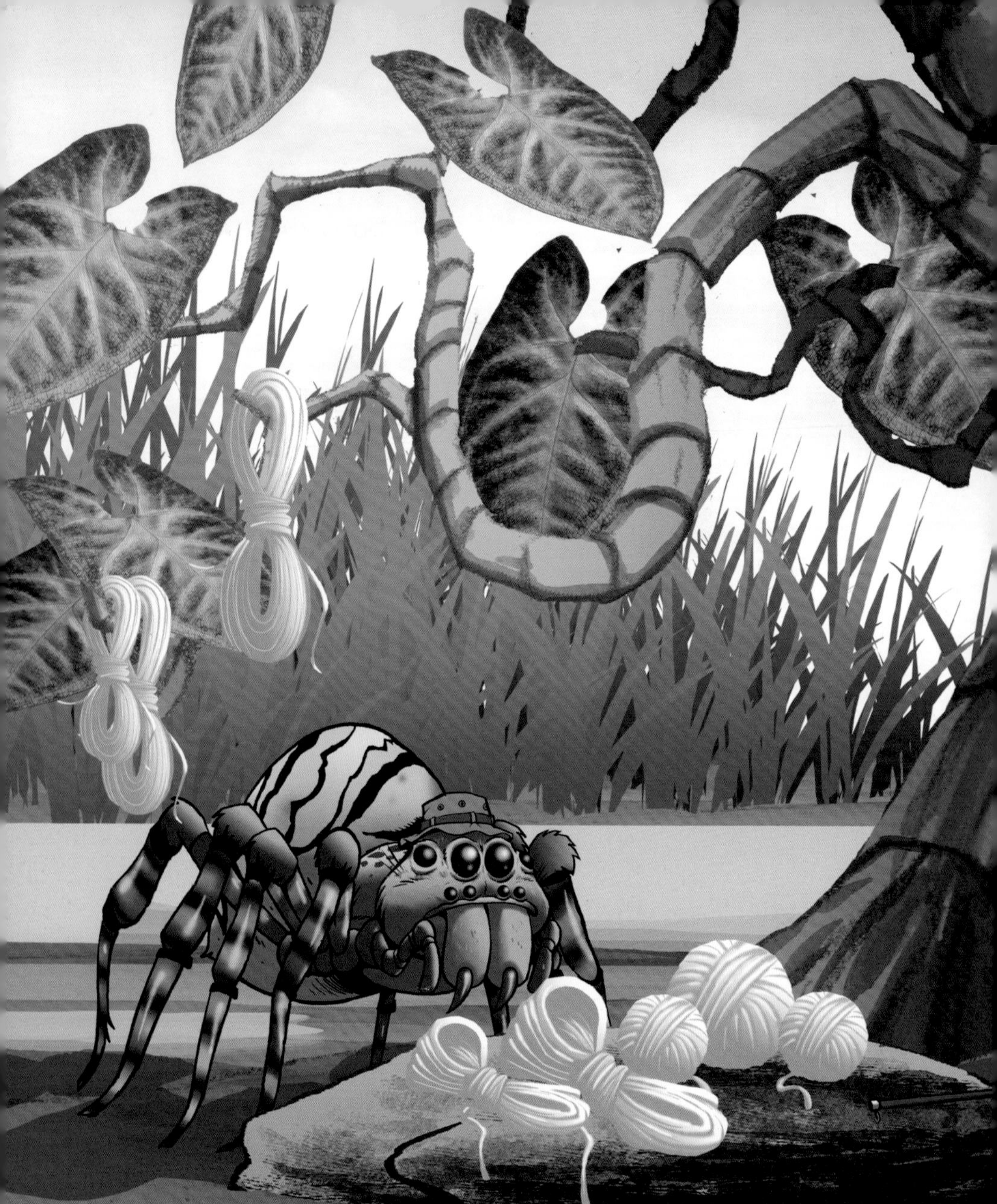

Spiders are just like silk factories. They can create up to seven different types of threads, like dry threads and threads soaked with a sticky matter.

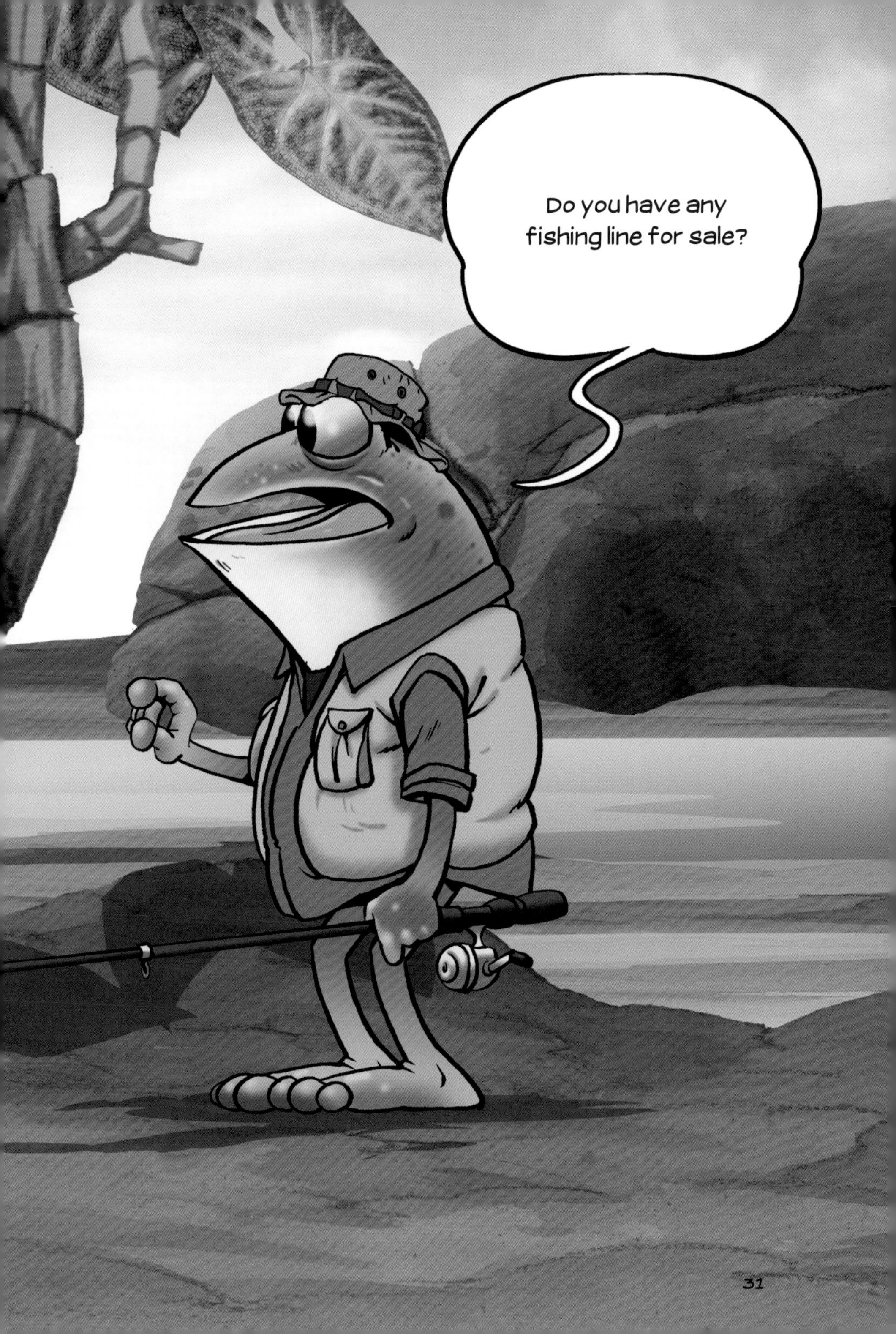
Do you have any fishing line for sale?

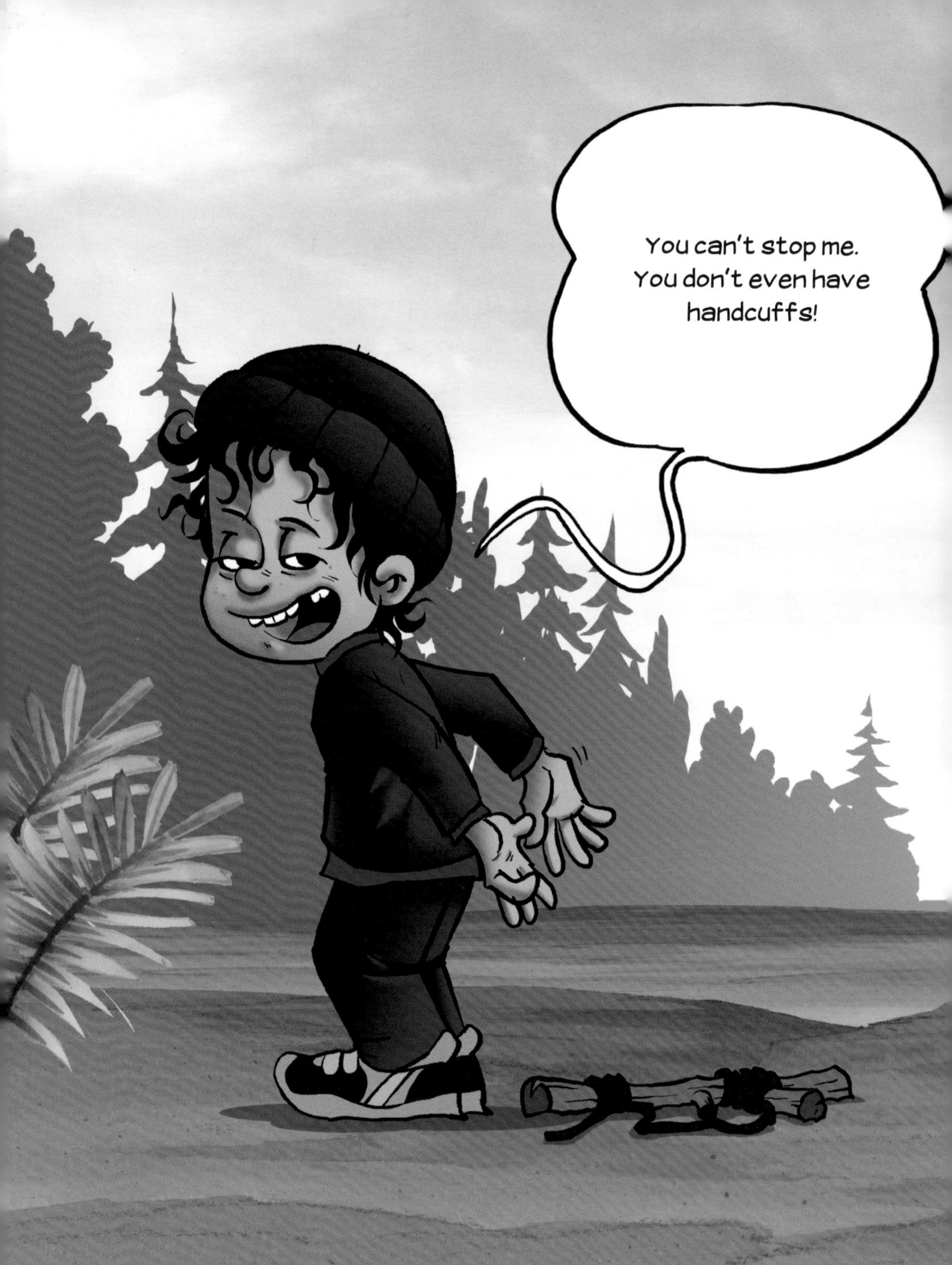
You can't stop me. You don't even have handcuffs!

A spider's silk is of higher quality than all man-made fibres. The most solid spider silk is 60 times more resistant than nylon.

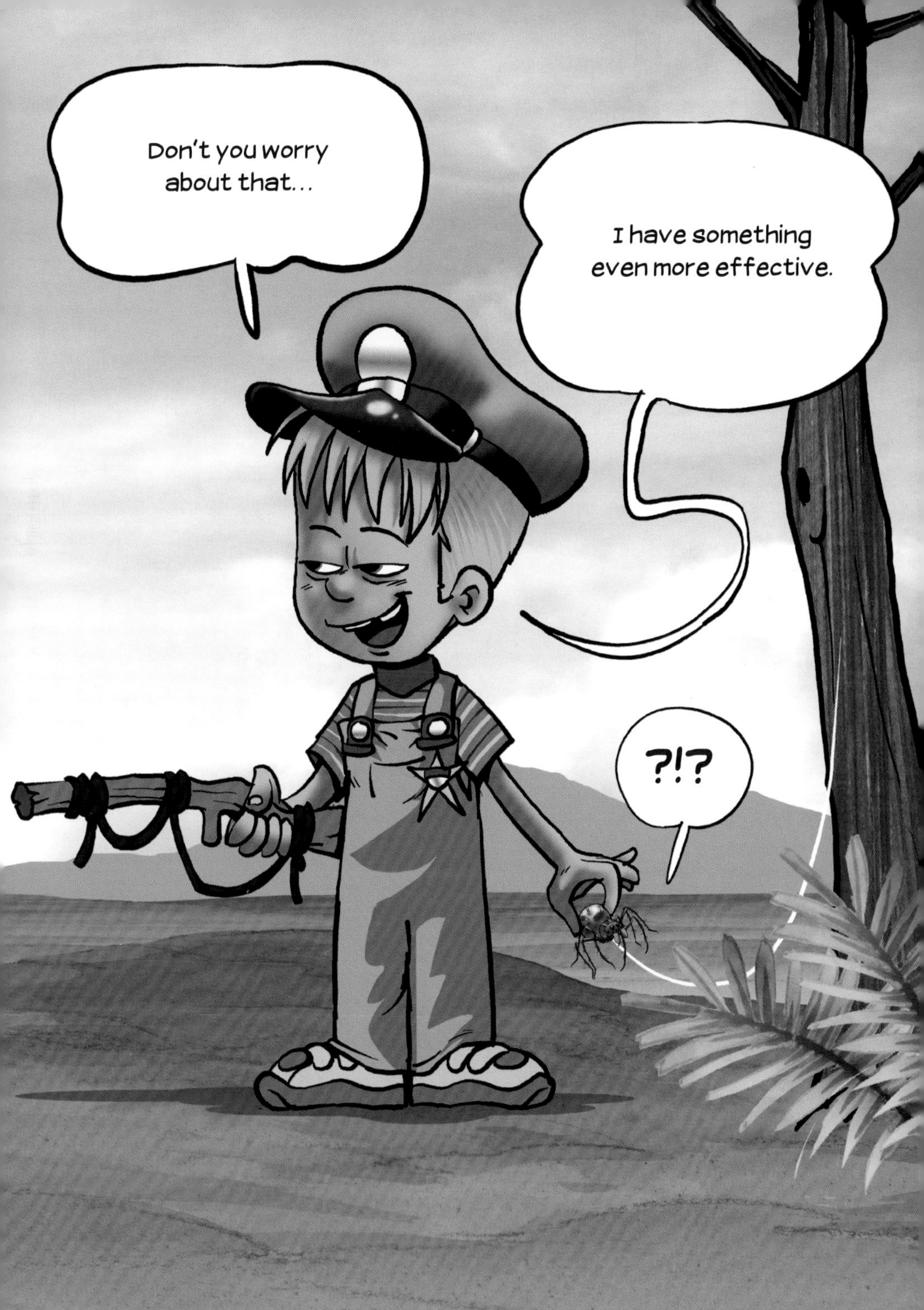
Don't you worry about that...
I have something even more effective.
?!?

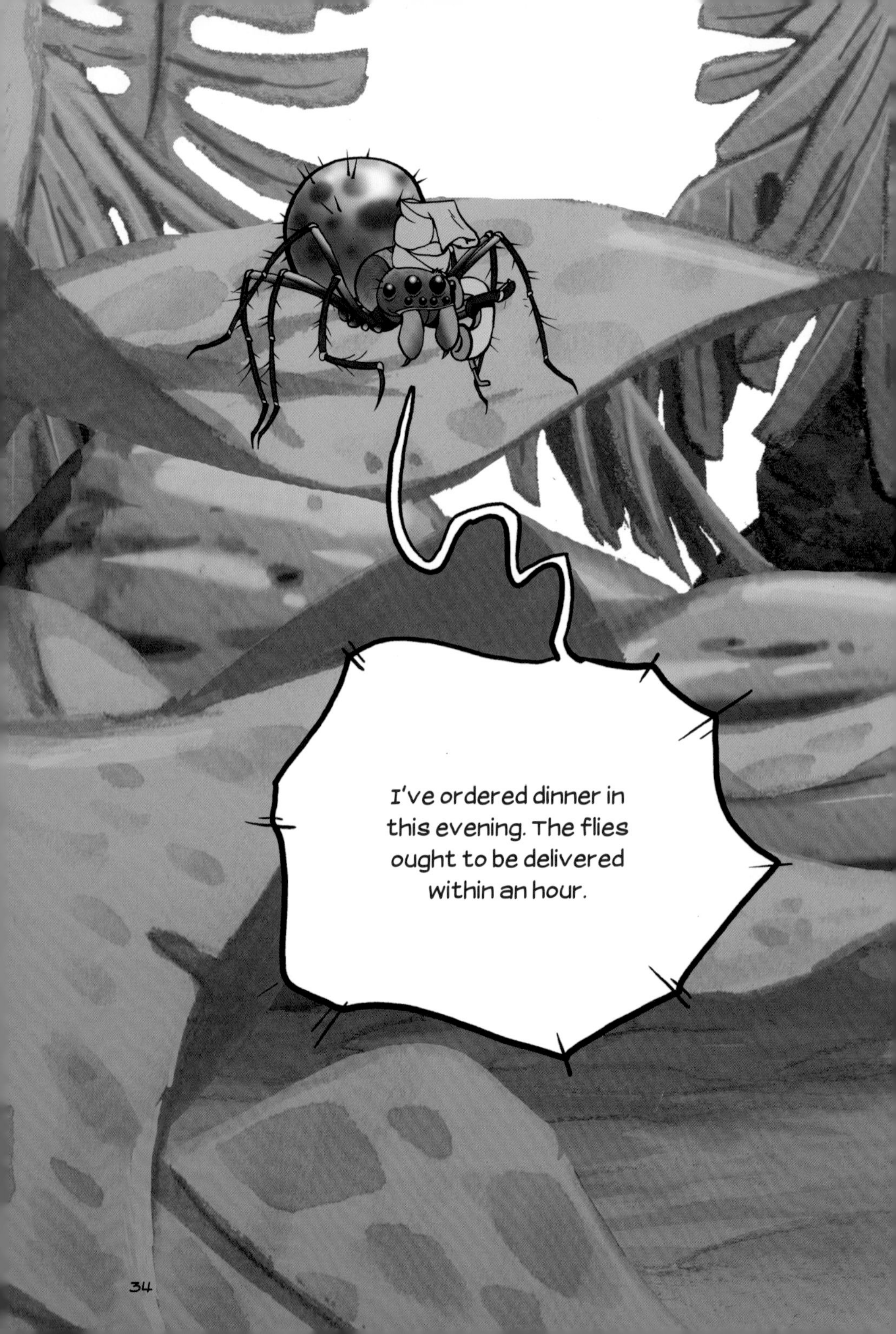
I've ordered dinner in this evening. The flies ought to be delivered within an hour.

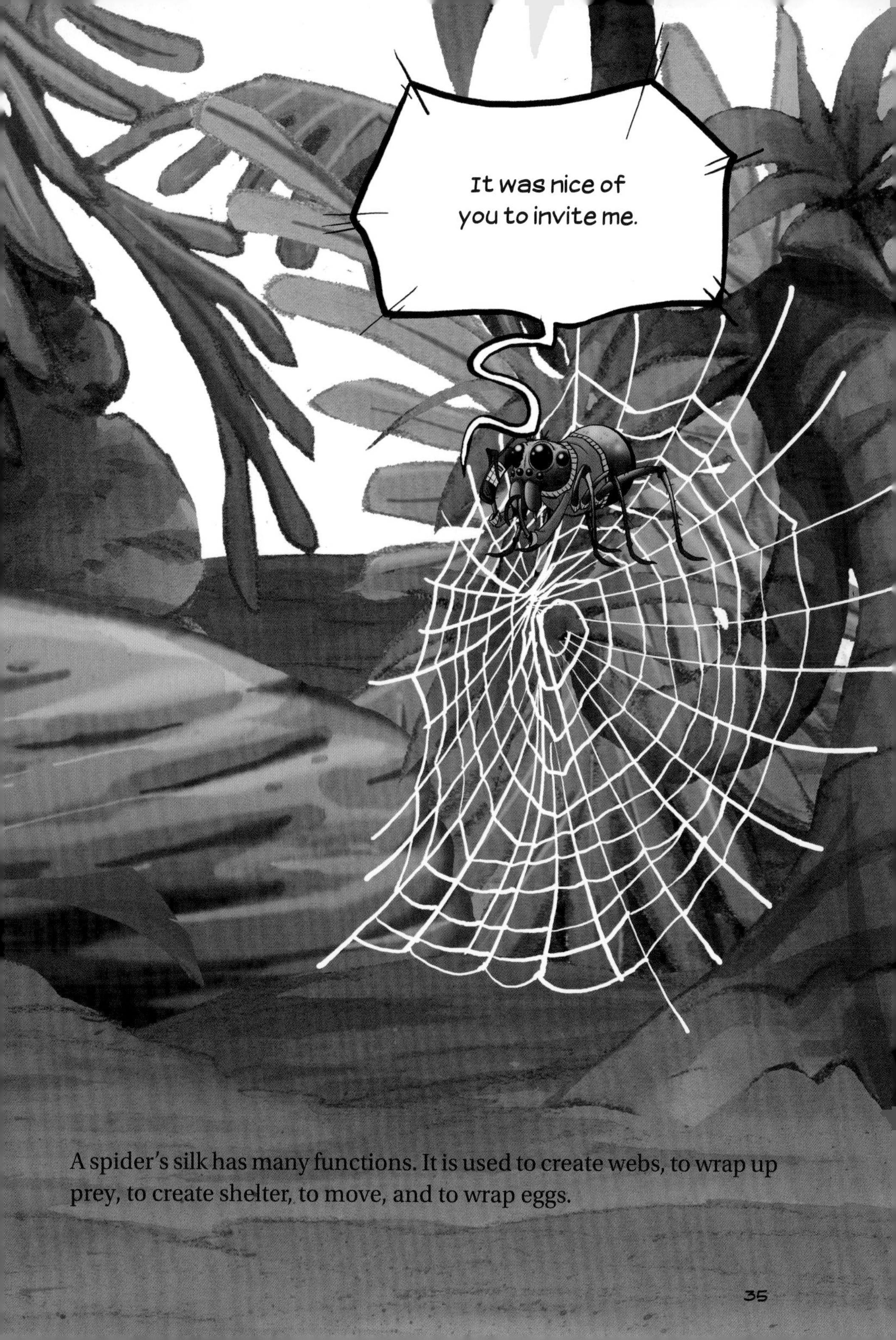
It was nice of you to invite me.

A spider's silk has many functions. It is used to create webs, to wrap up prey, to create shelter, to move, and to wrap eggs.

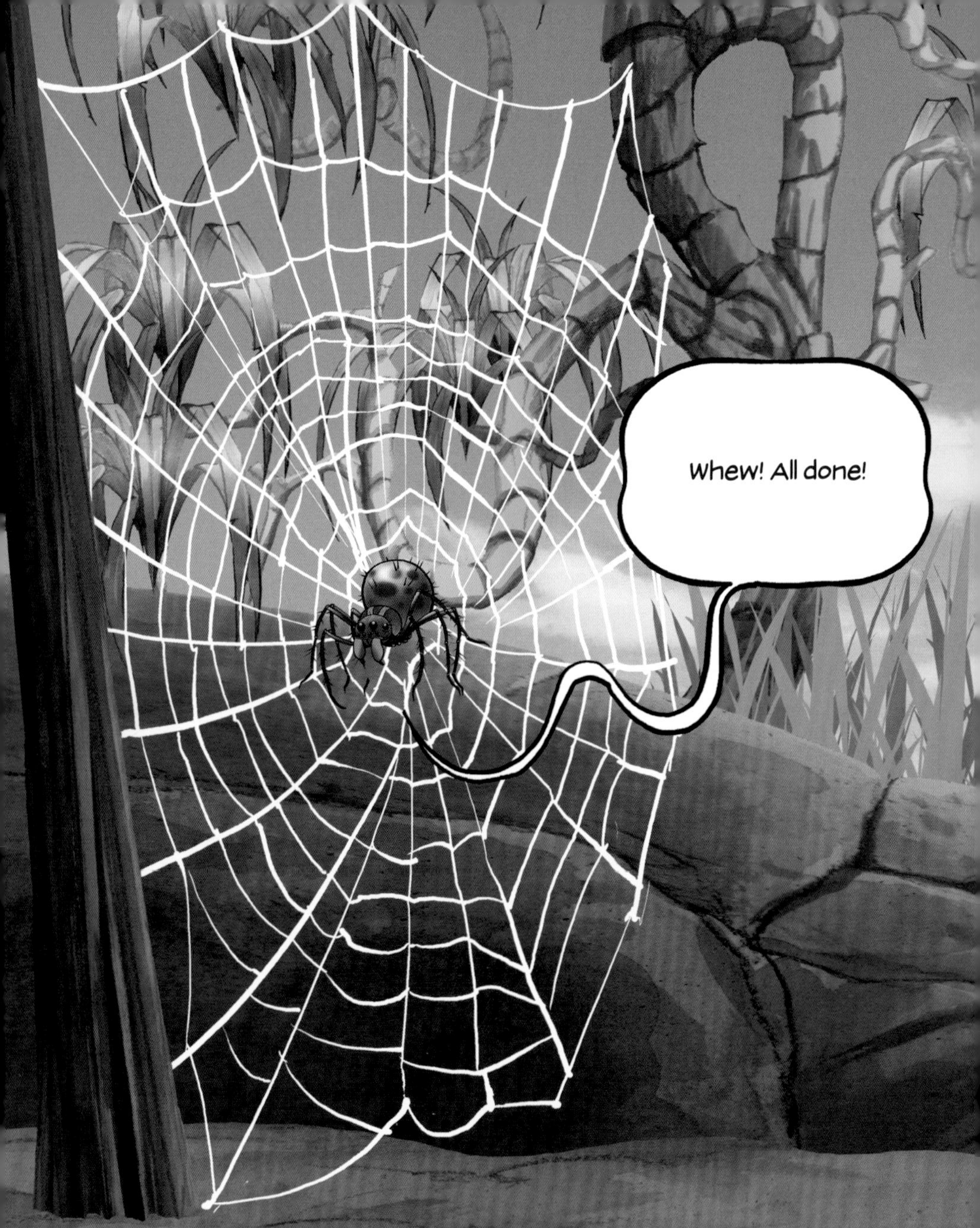
Whew! All done!

Spiders that weave their webs in a geometric shape reconstruct a new web each night. The reconstruction generally takes about an hour to complete.

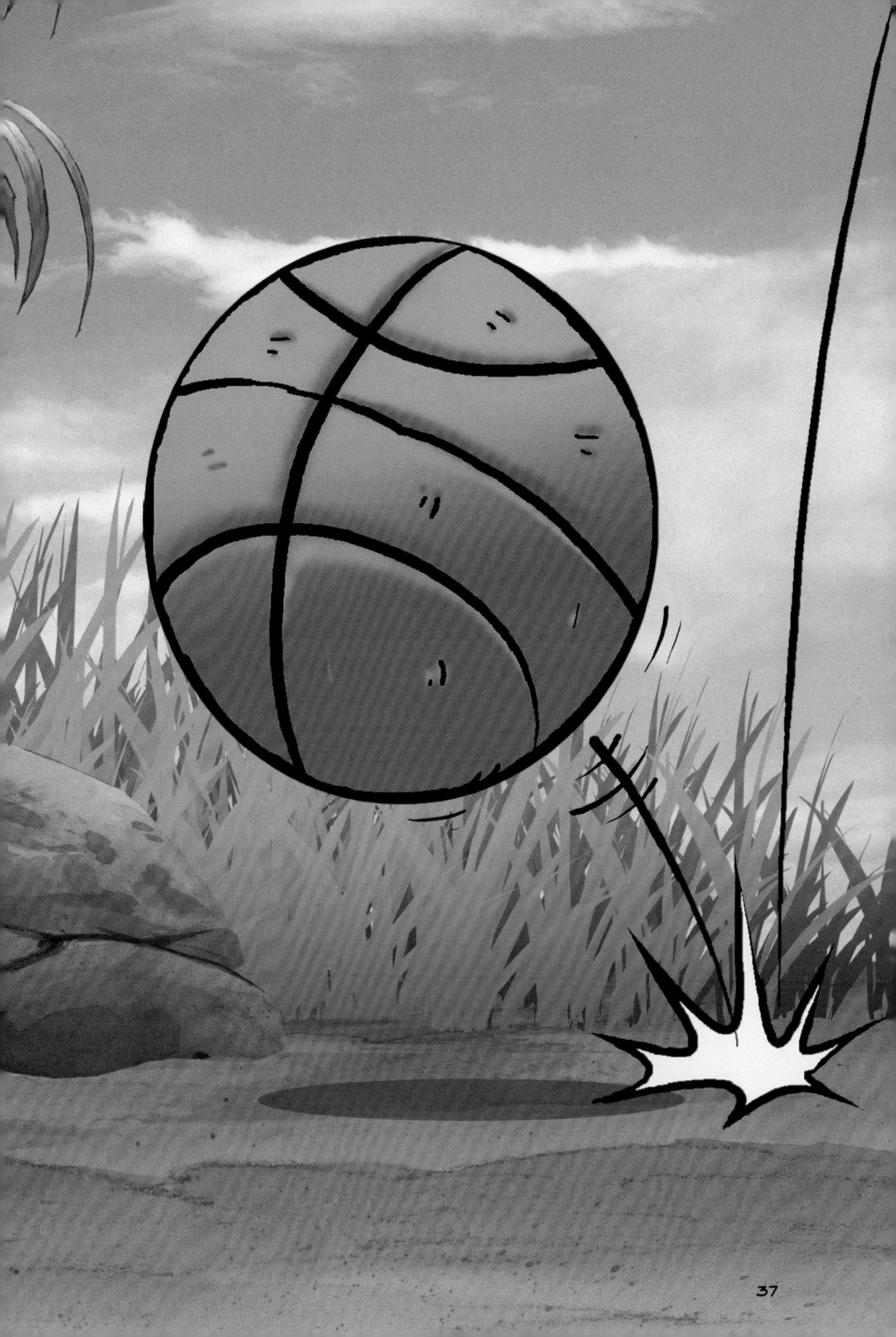

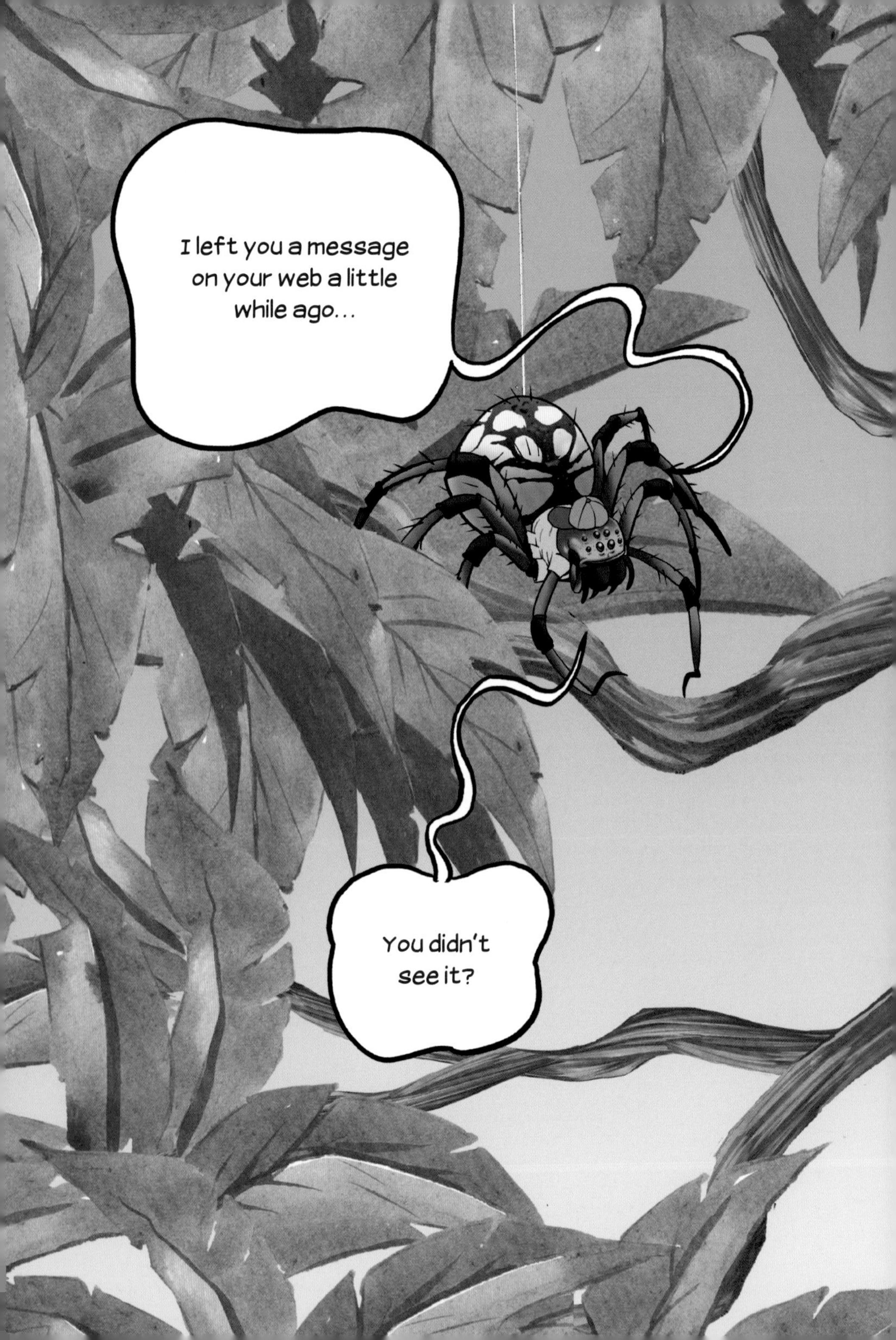
I left you a message on your web a little while ago...
You didn't see it?

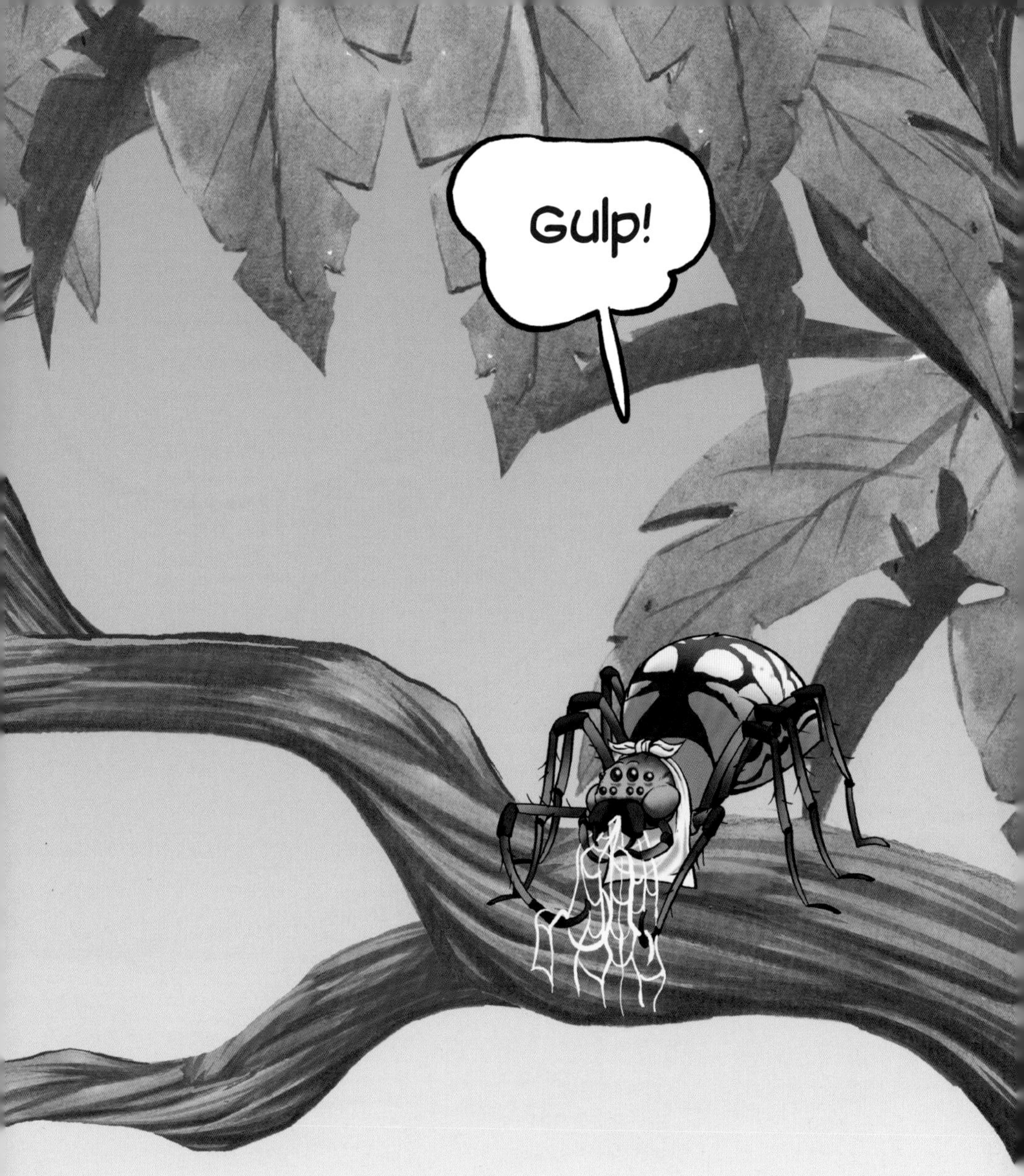
Gulp!

Before constructing its new web, a spider will eat its old web. It recovers a lot of protein by eating it.

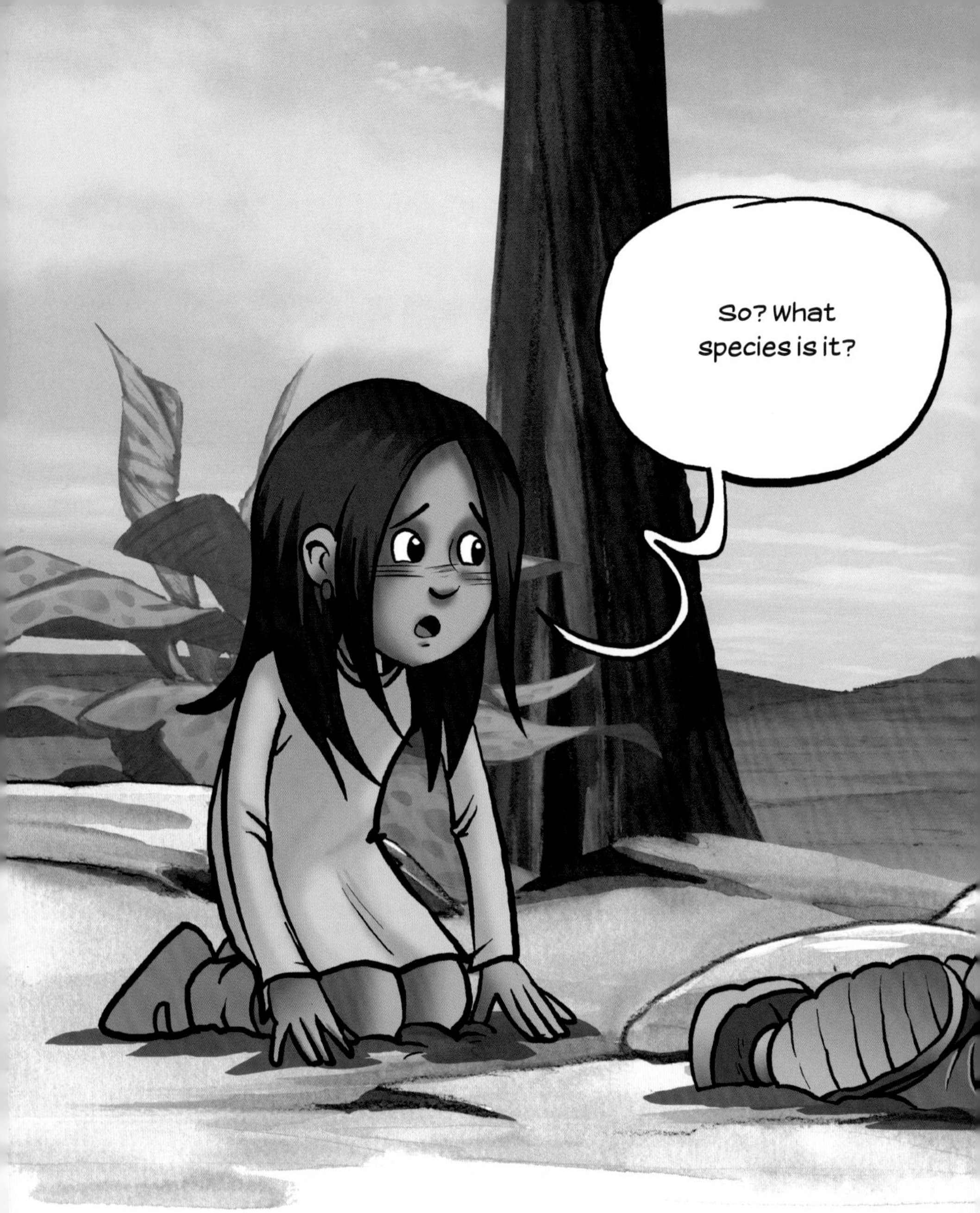
So? What species is it?

A spider's web indicates what type of species it is.

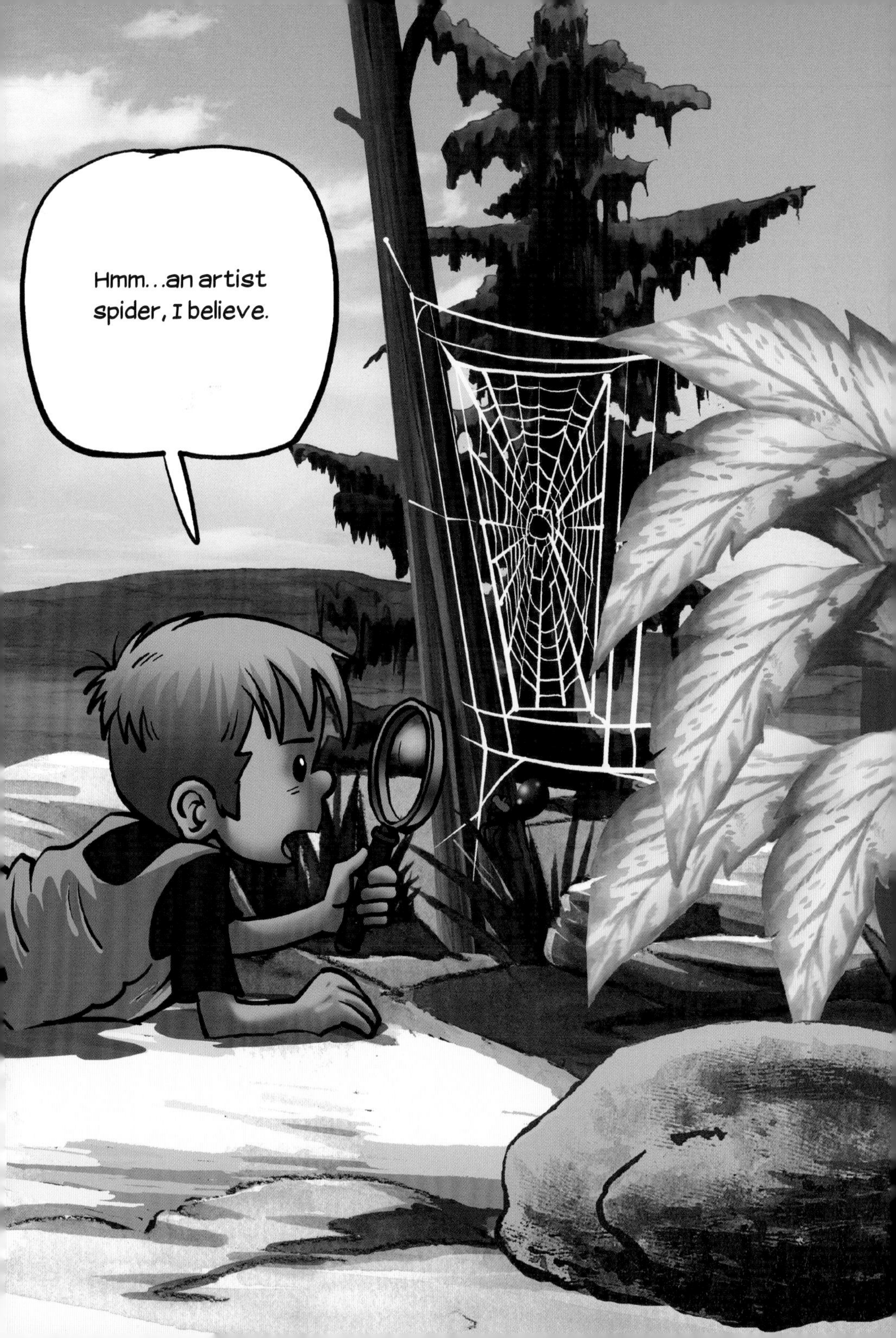
Hmm...an artist spider, I believe.

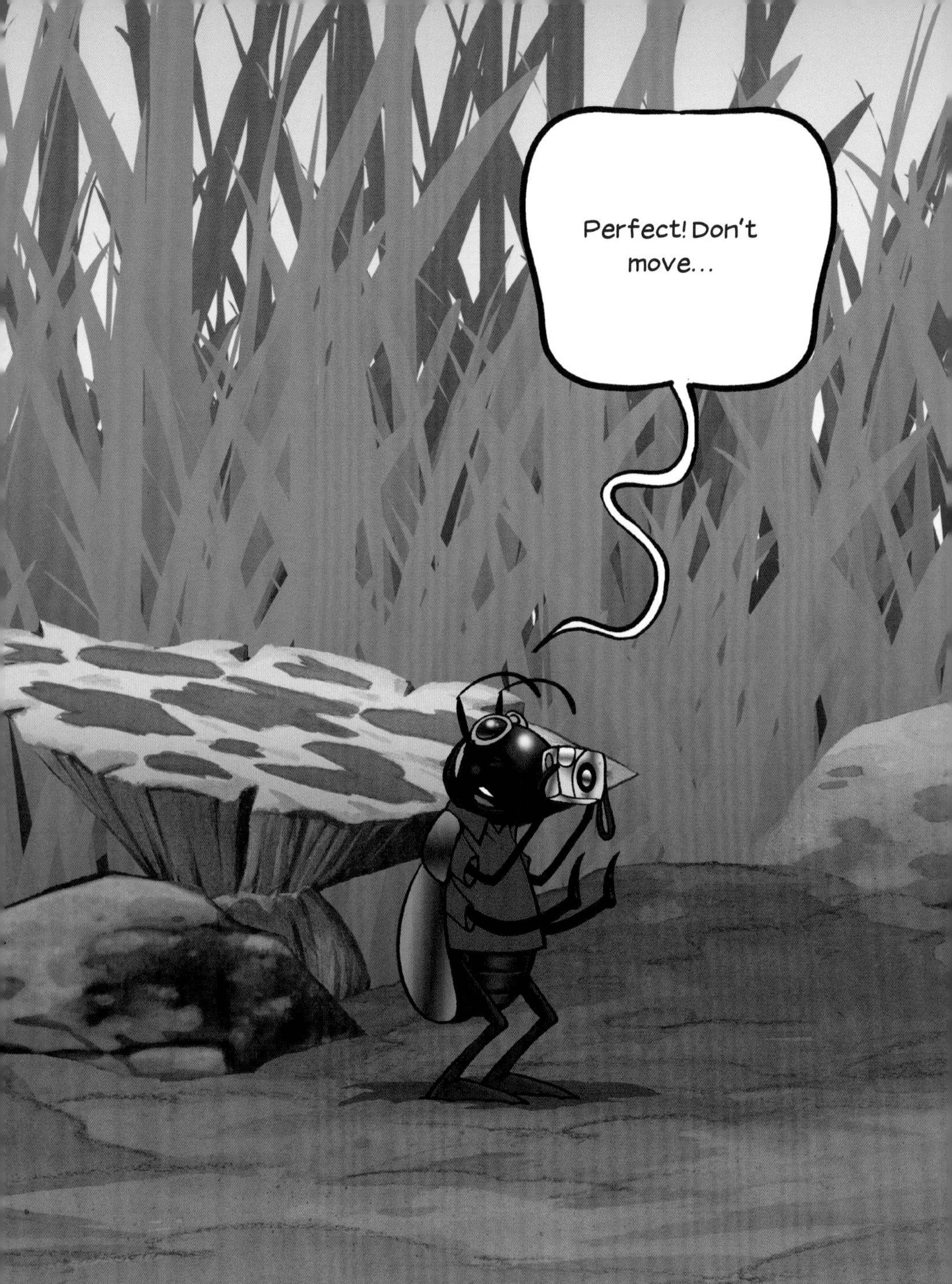
Perfect! Don't move...

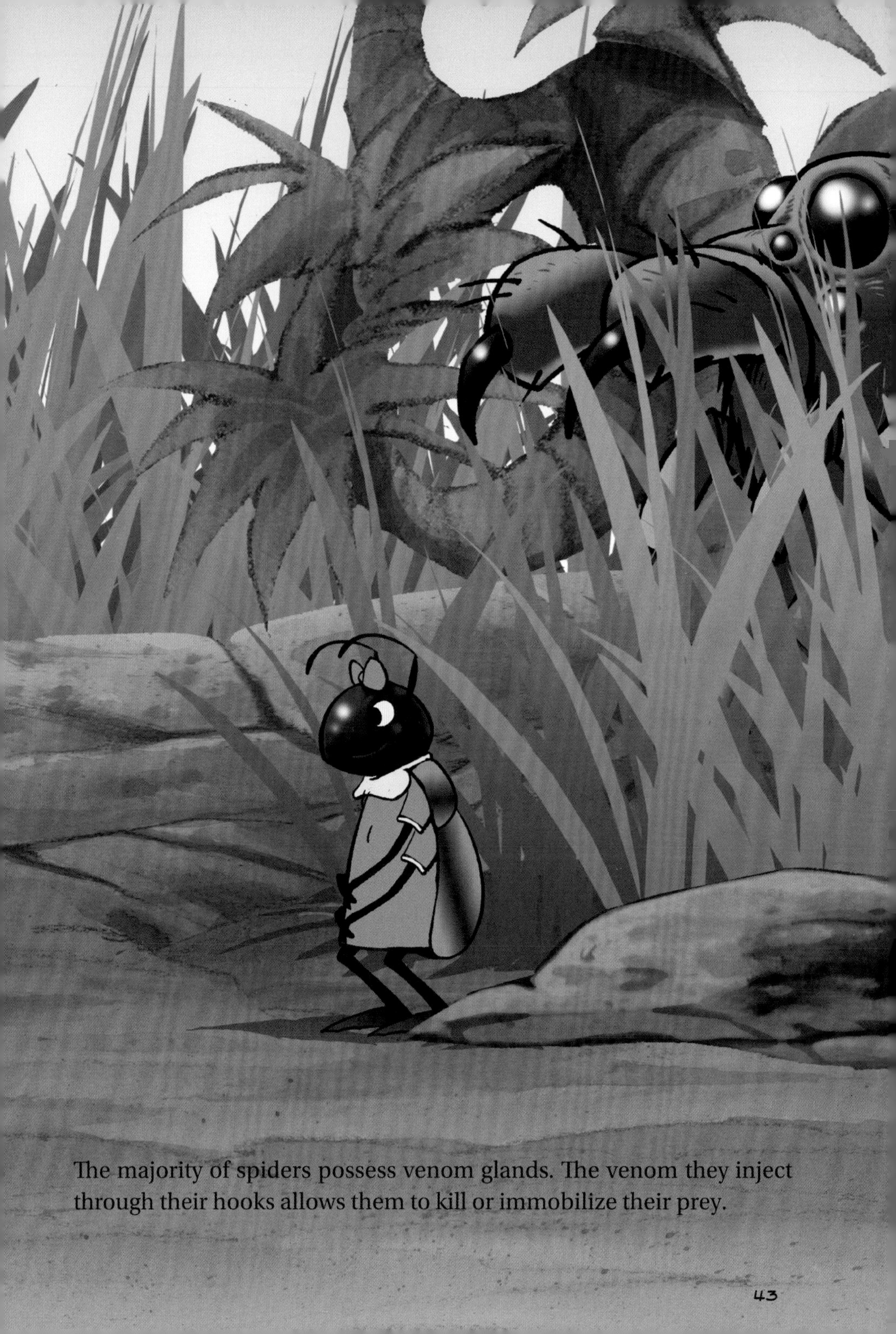

The majority of spiders possess venom glands. The venom they inject through their hooks allows them to kill or immobilize their prey.

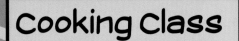

Cooking Class

> Remember to wrap the insect very tightly before injecting the venom.

Once spiders capture their prey, they wrap it up tightly in thread. Then, they inject it with a strong liquid that will soften the inside of its body until it becomes liquid.

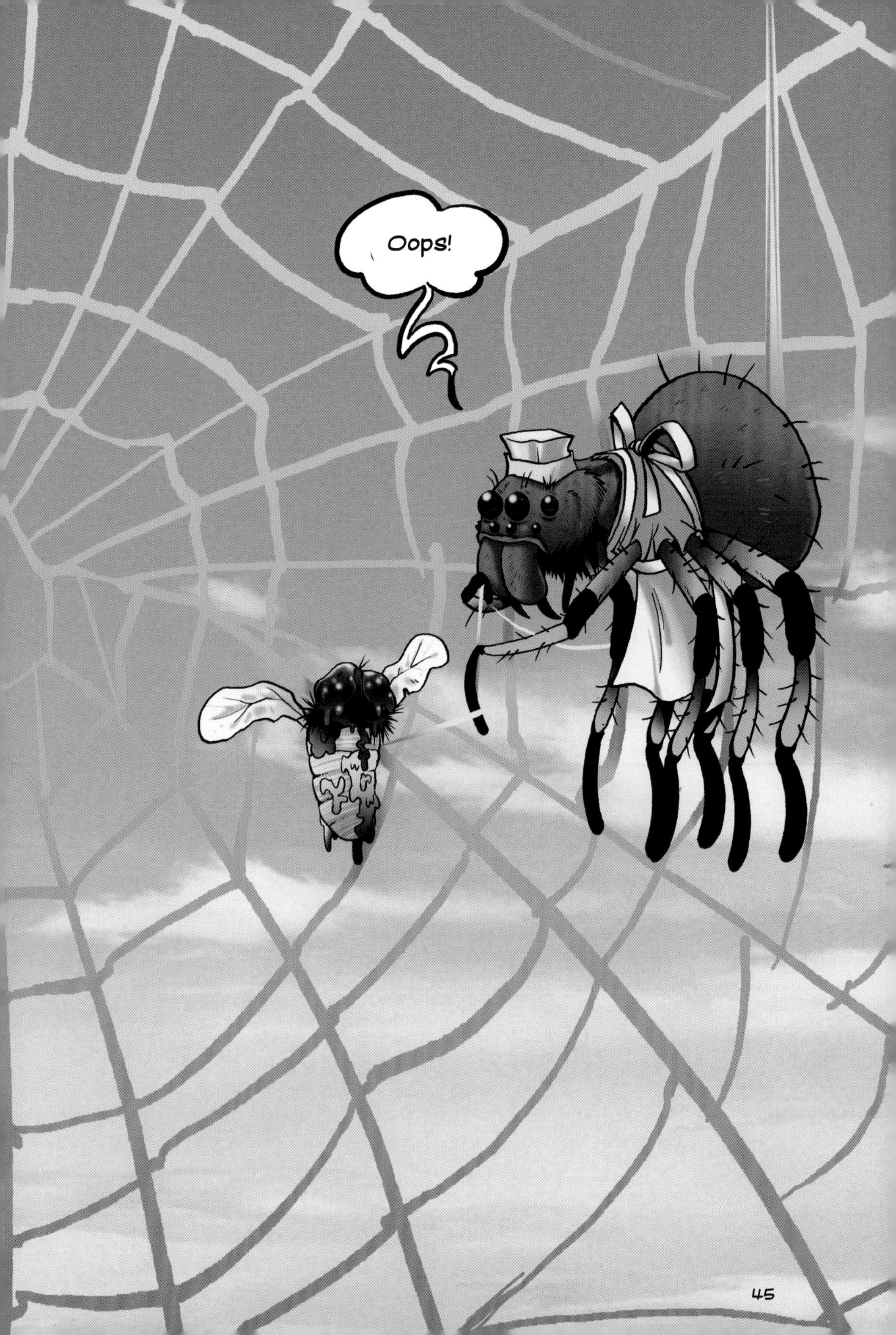
Oops!

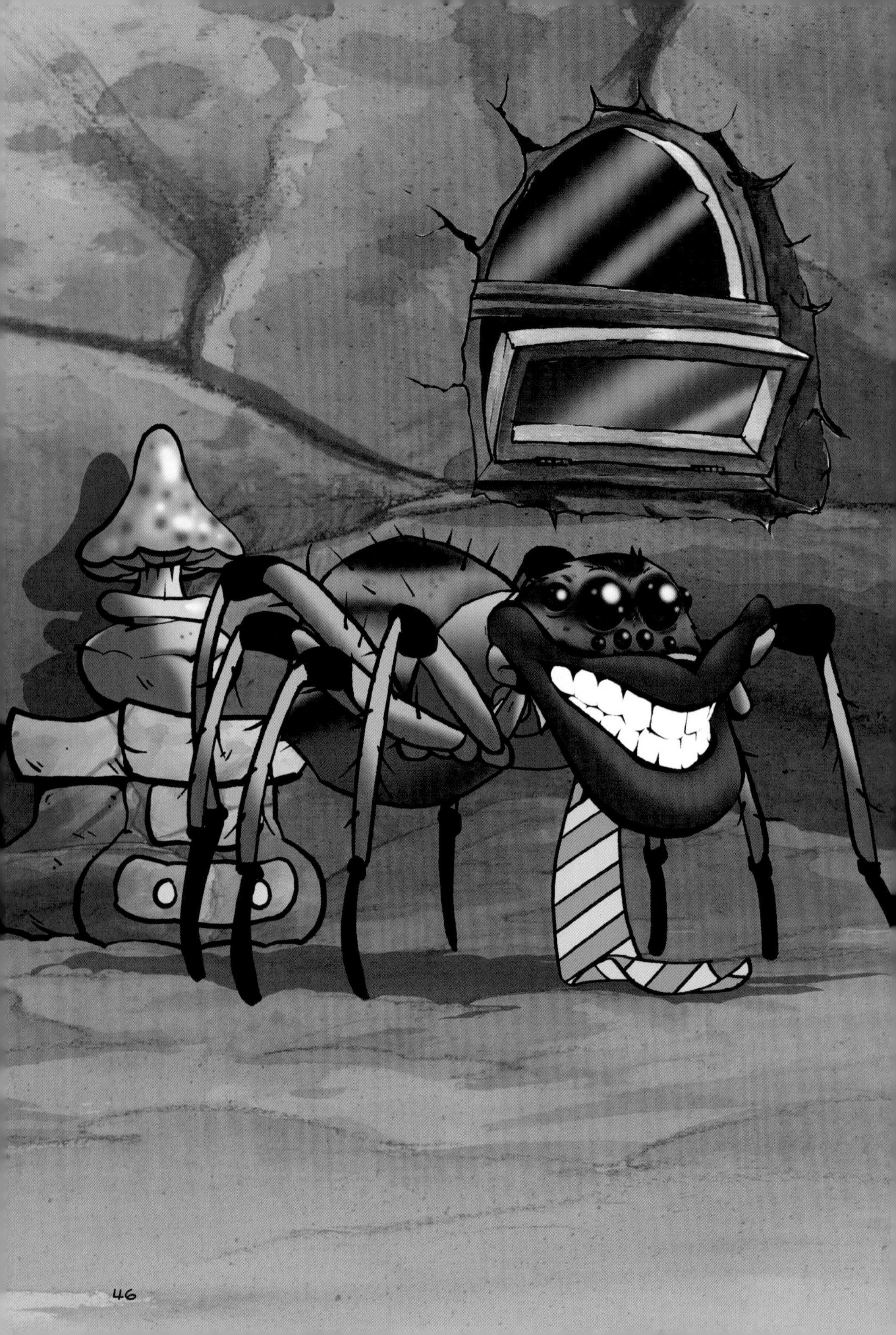

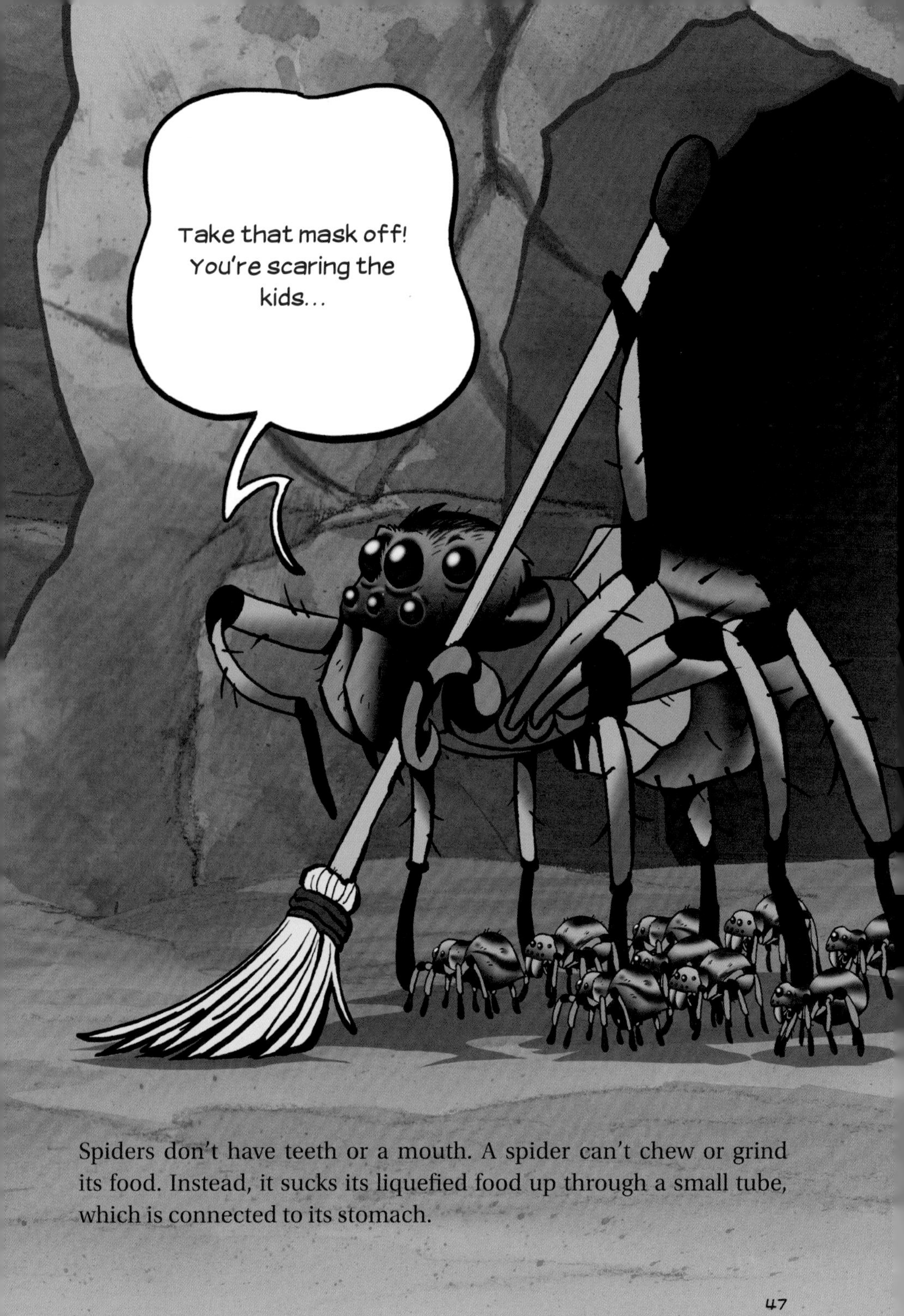
Take that mask off! You're scaring the kids...

Spiders don't have teeth or a mouth. A spider can't chew or grind its food. Instead, it sucks its liquefied food up through a small tube, which is connected to its stomach.

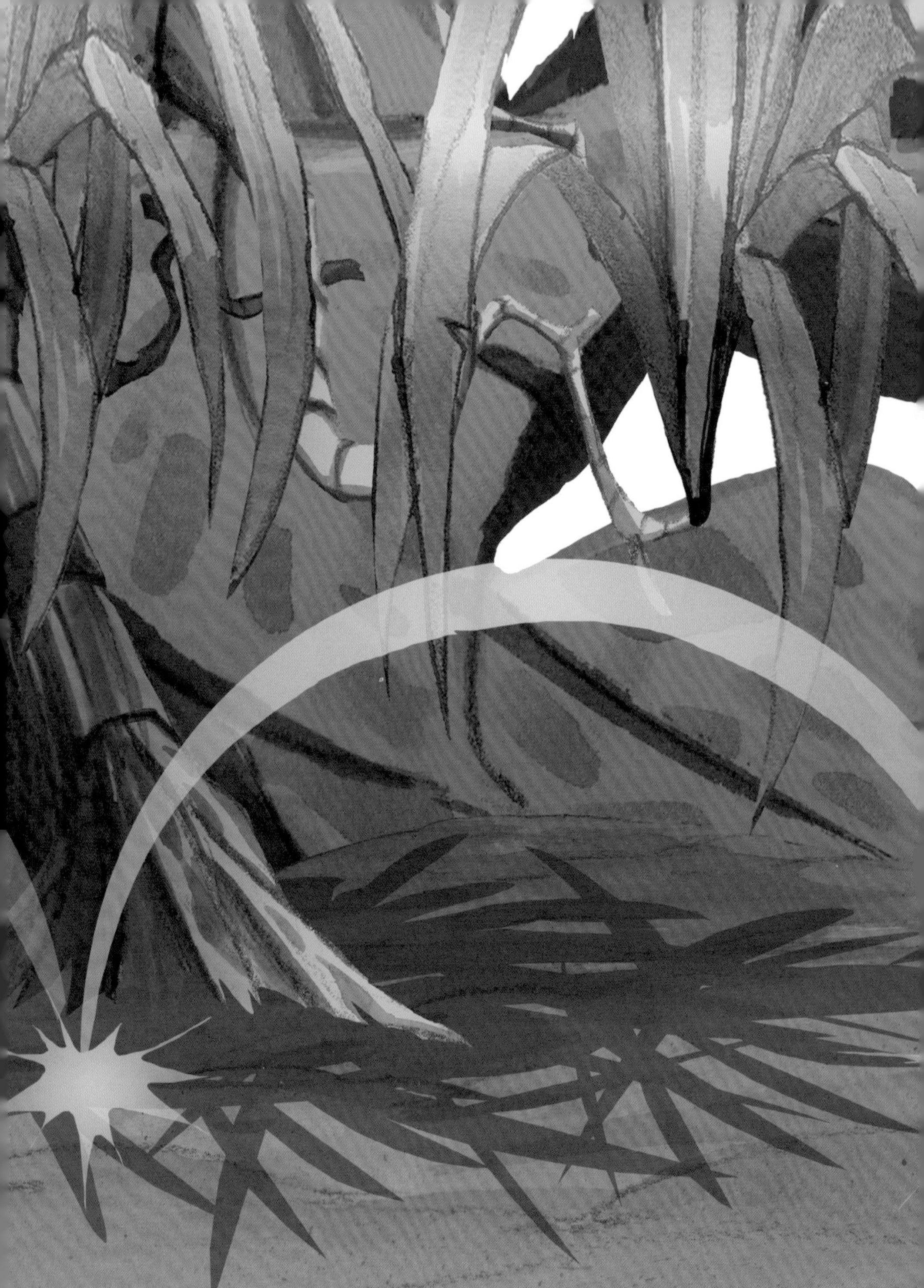

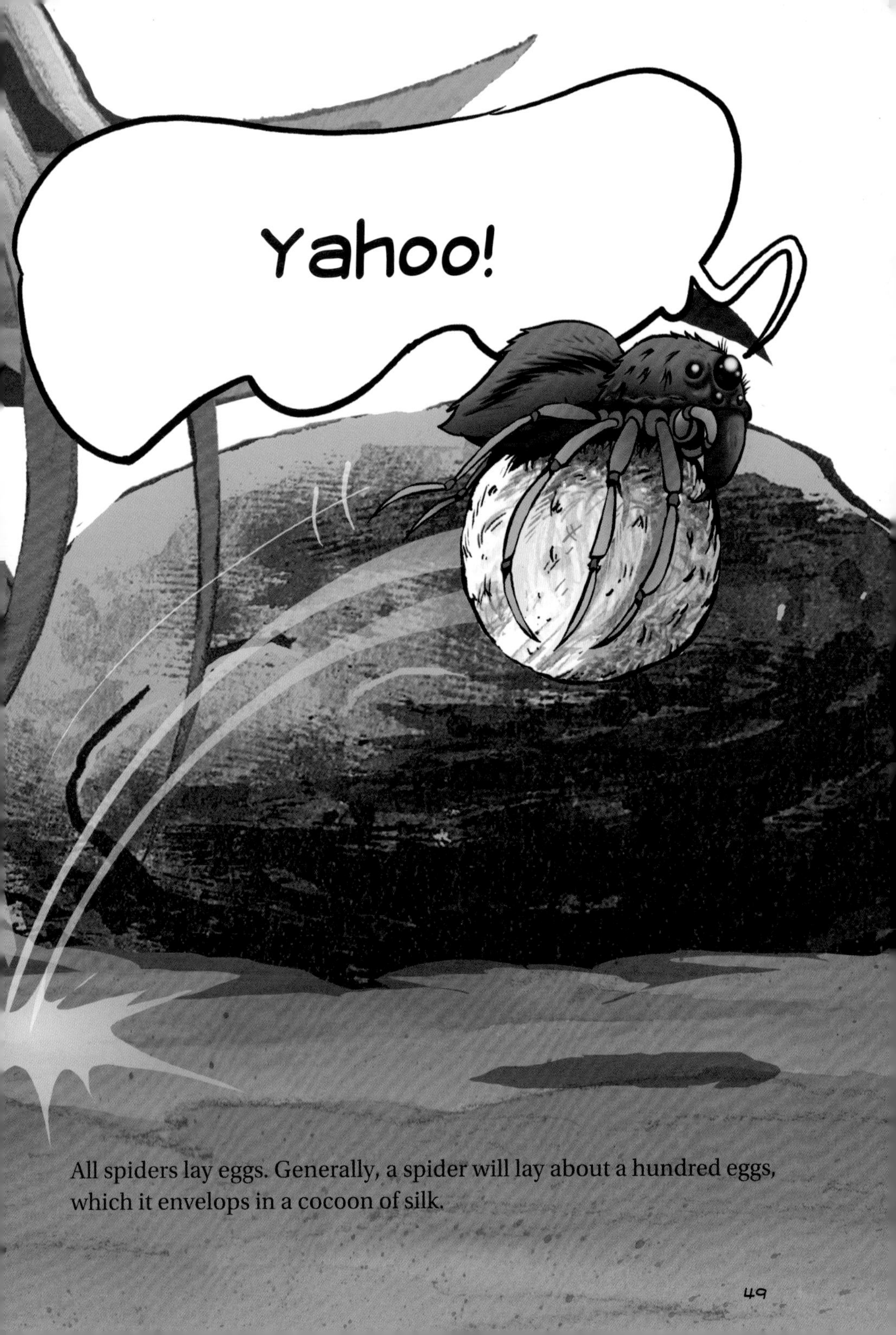
Yahoo!

All spiders lay eggs. Generally, a spider will lay about a hundred eggs, which it envelops in a cocoon of silk.

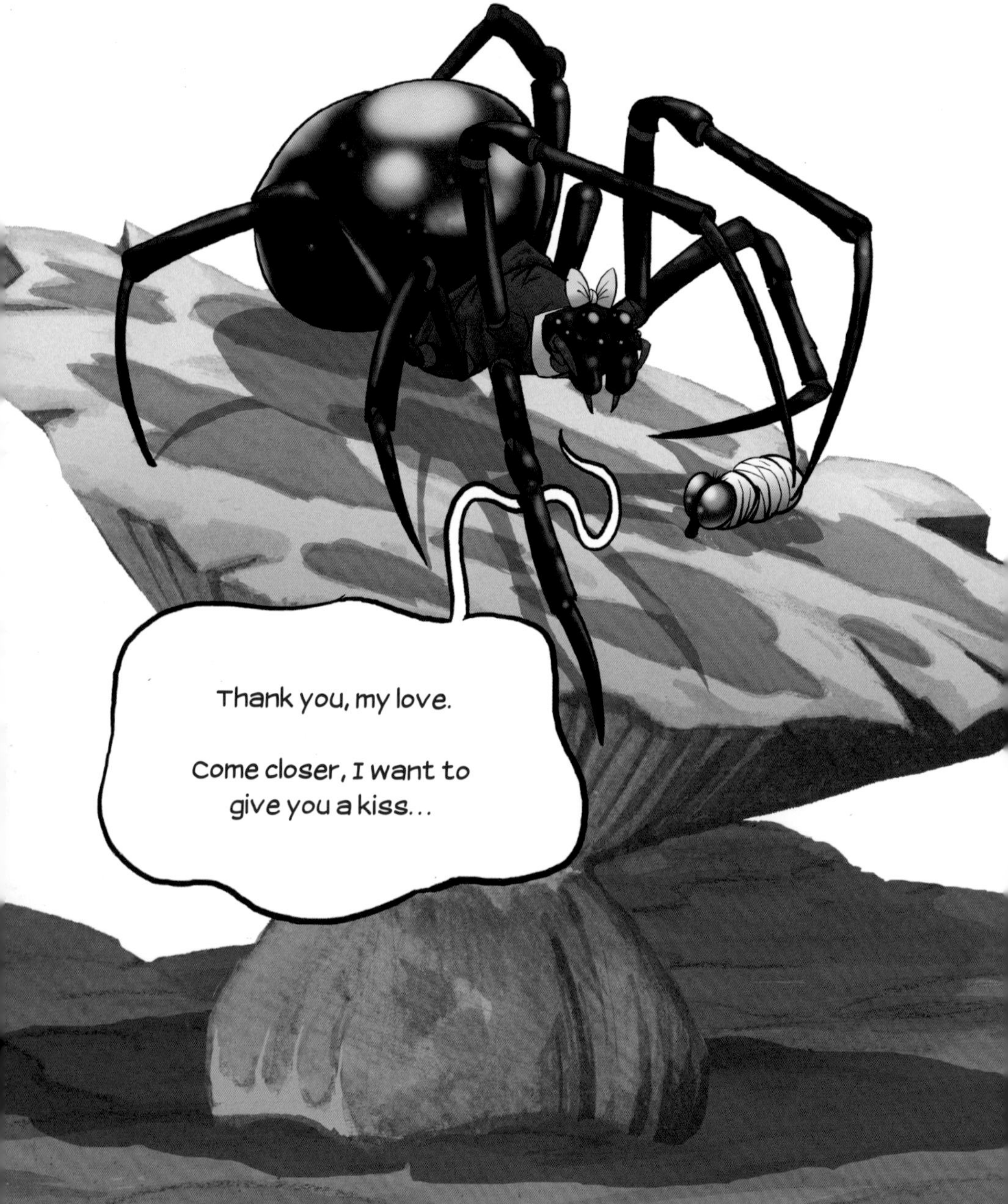
Thank you, my love.
Come closer, I want to give you a kiss...

While mating, the male must always be on guard. At any moment, the female could kill and eat him. Within certain species, the male will offer the female a fly as a gift in an attempt to escape death.

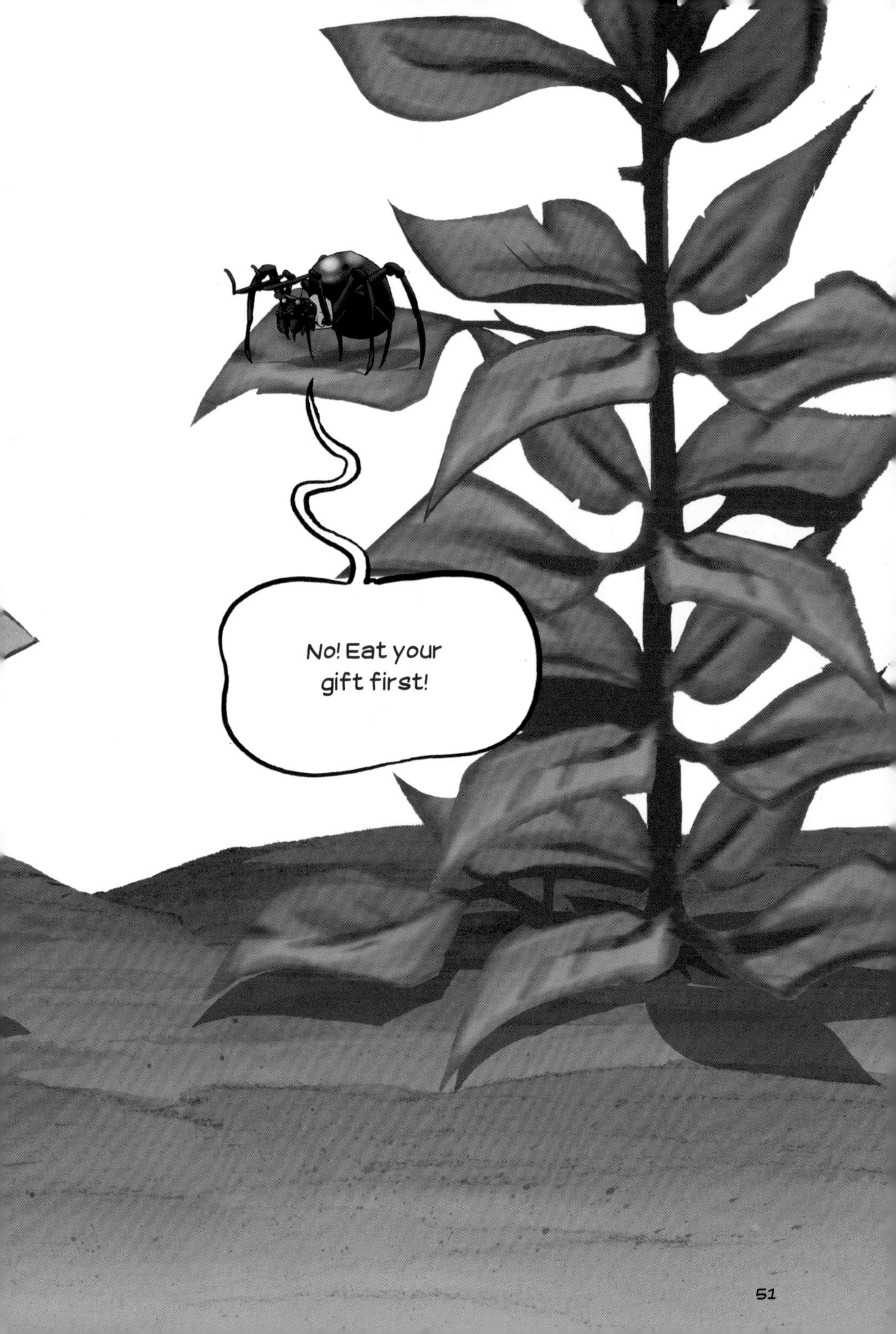
No! Eat your gift first!

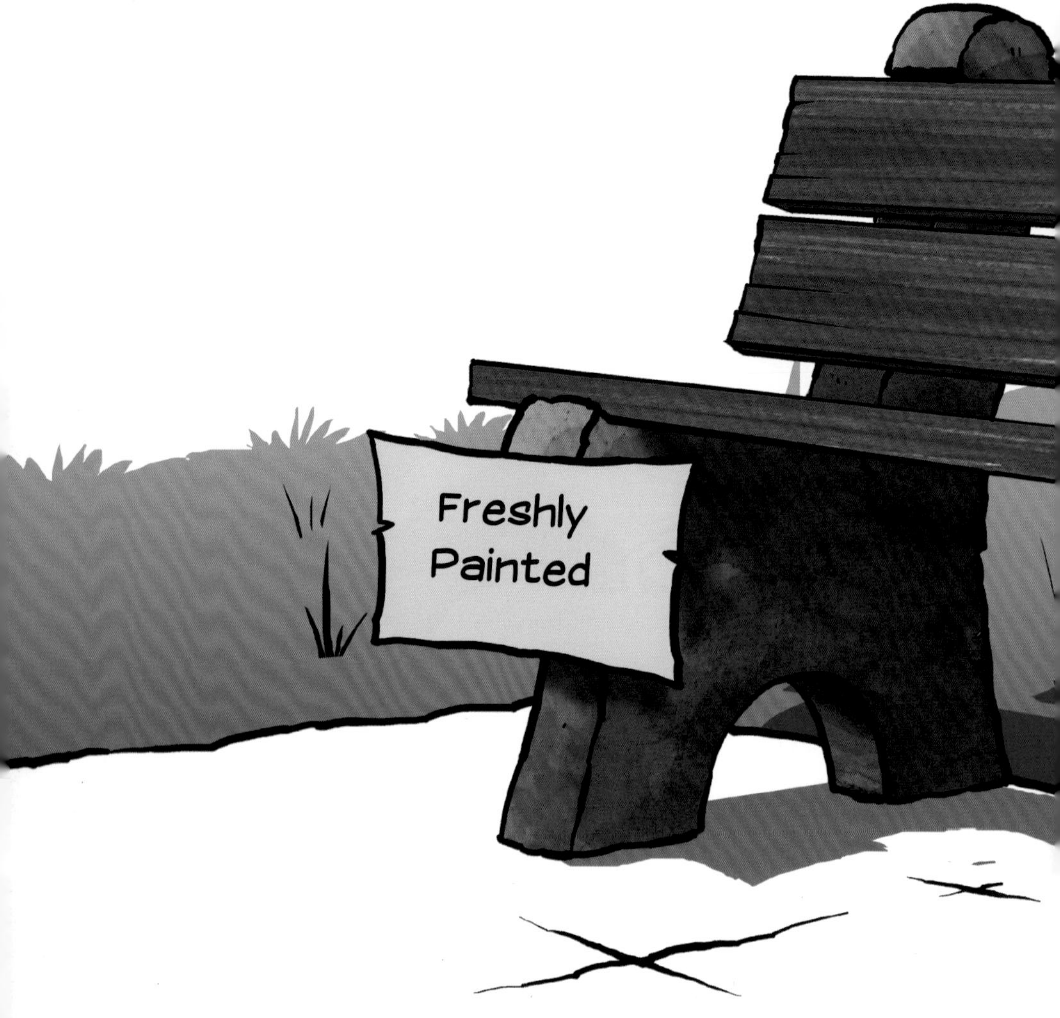
Freshly
Painted

Depending on the species, some females abandon their eggs once they are laid. Others house and feed their young. Some will even transport their babies, ten at a time, clinging onto their backs.

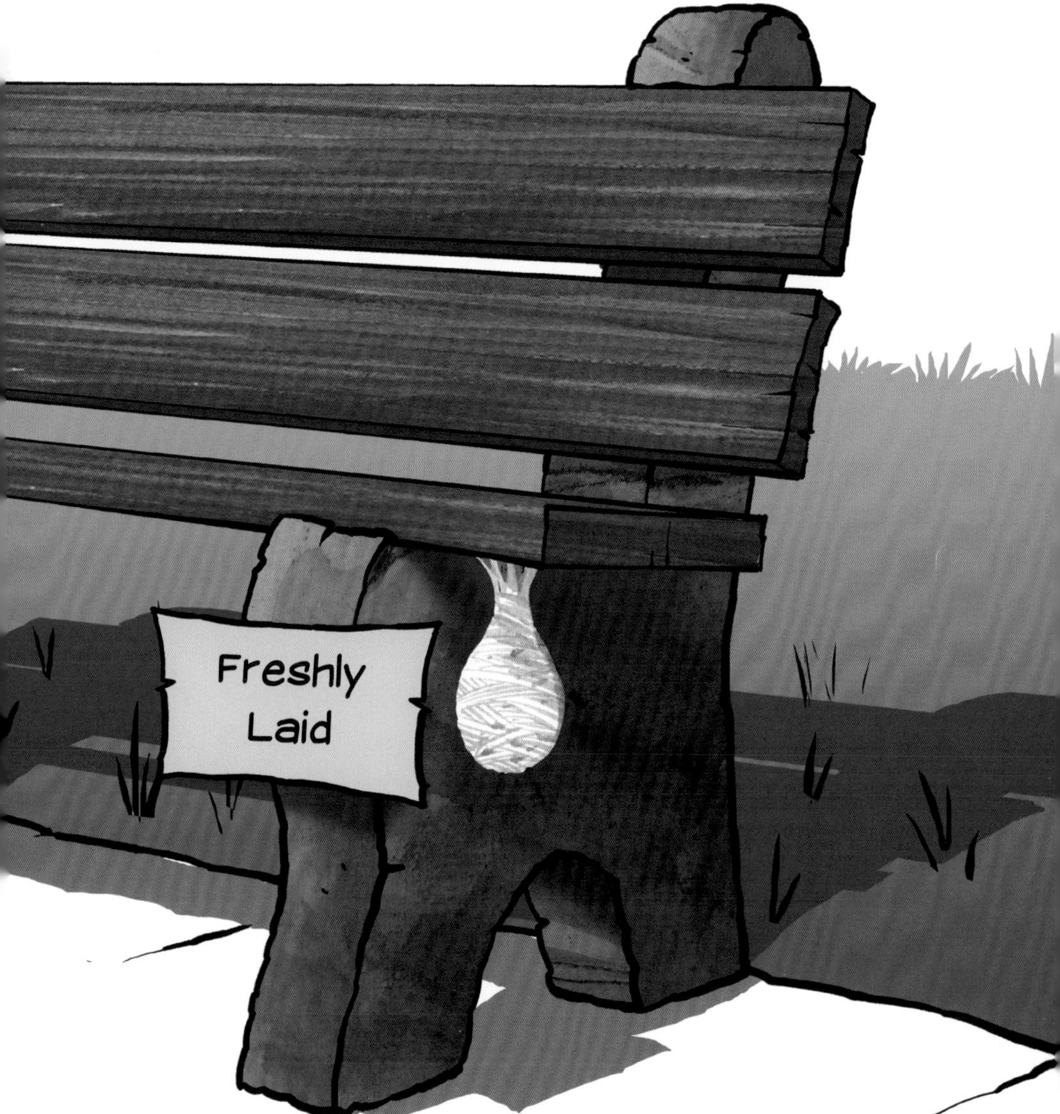
Freshly
Laid

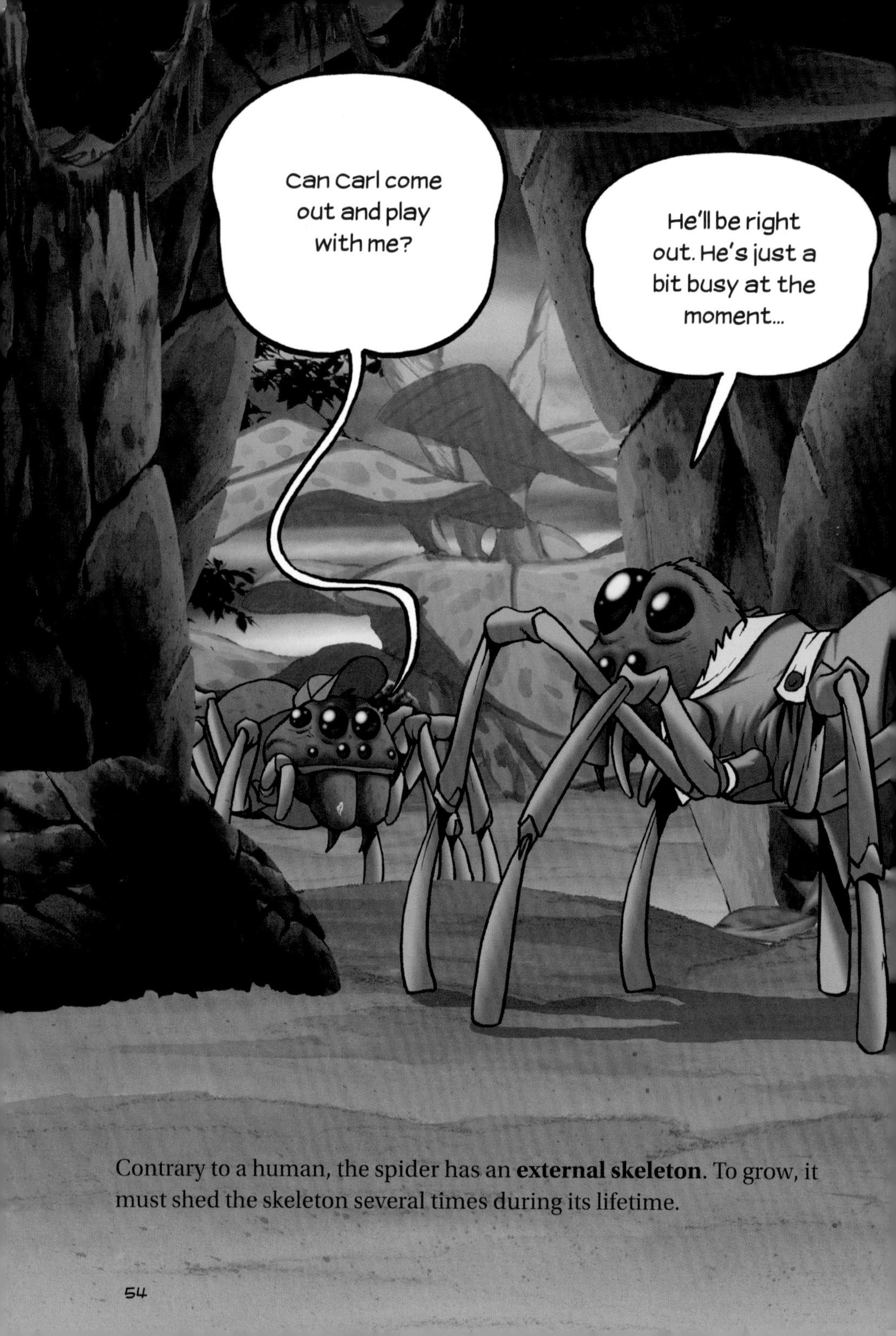
Can Carl come out and play with me?
He'll be right out. He's just a bit busy at the moment...

Contrary to a human, the spider has an **external skeleton**. To grow, it must shed the skeleton several times during its lifetime.

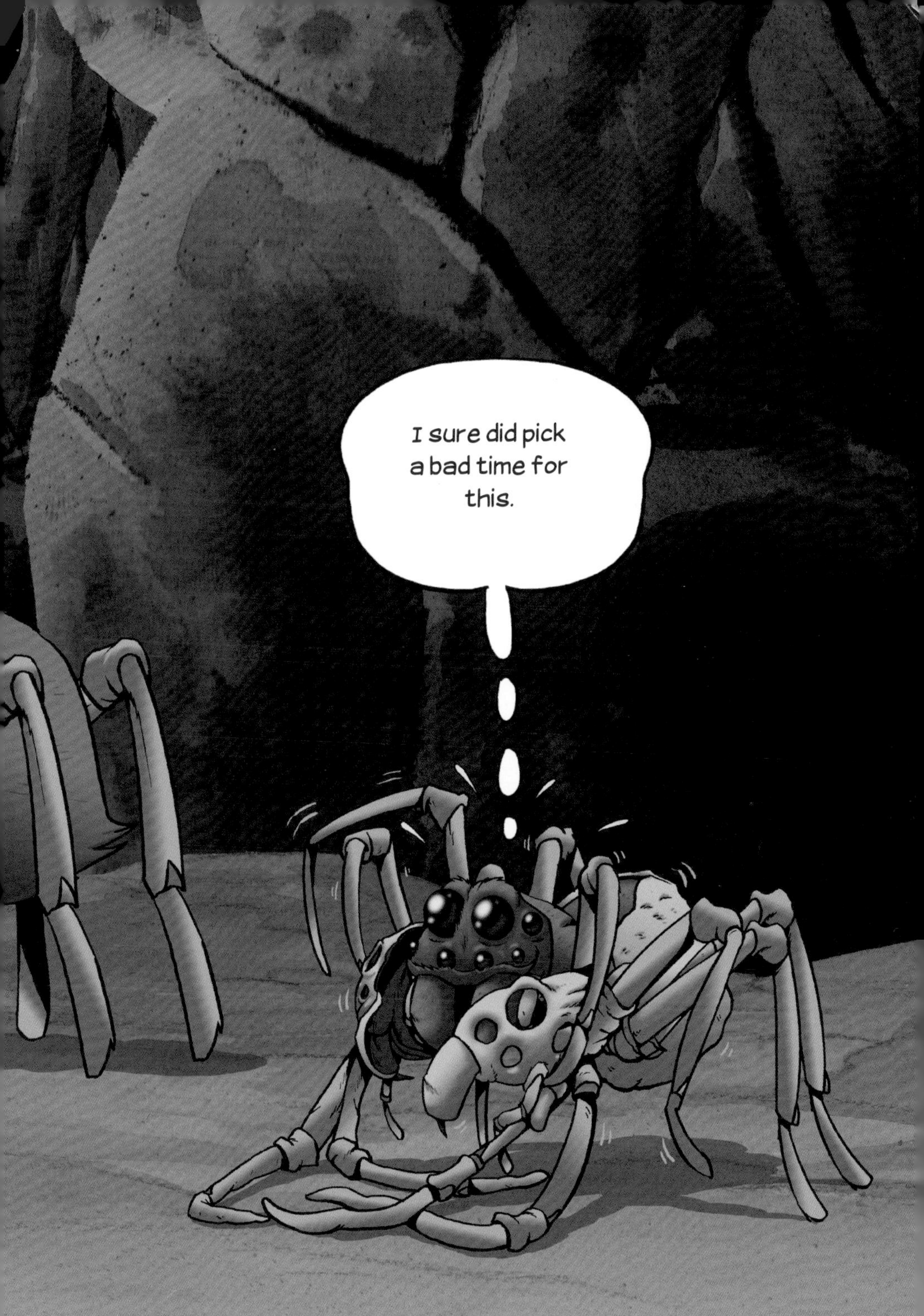
I sure did pick a bad time for this.

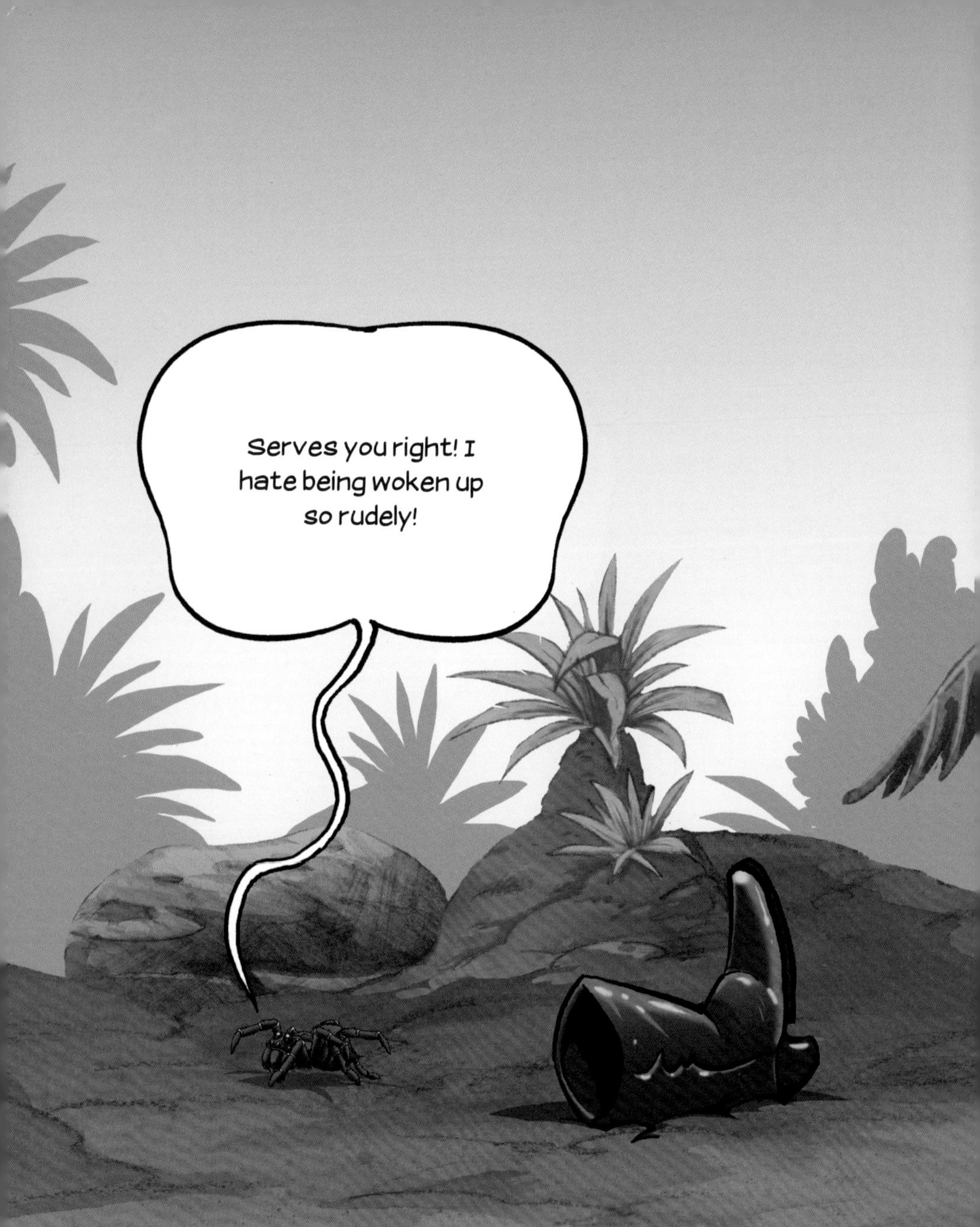
Serves you right! I hate being woken up so rudely!

Only a few species of spider are dangerous to humans. The most dangerous is a tarantula species found in Australia. Its venom is so powerful that it can kill an adult within a few hours.

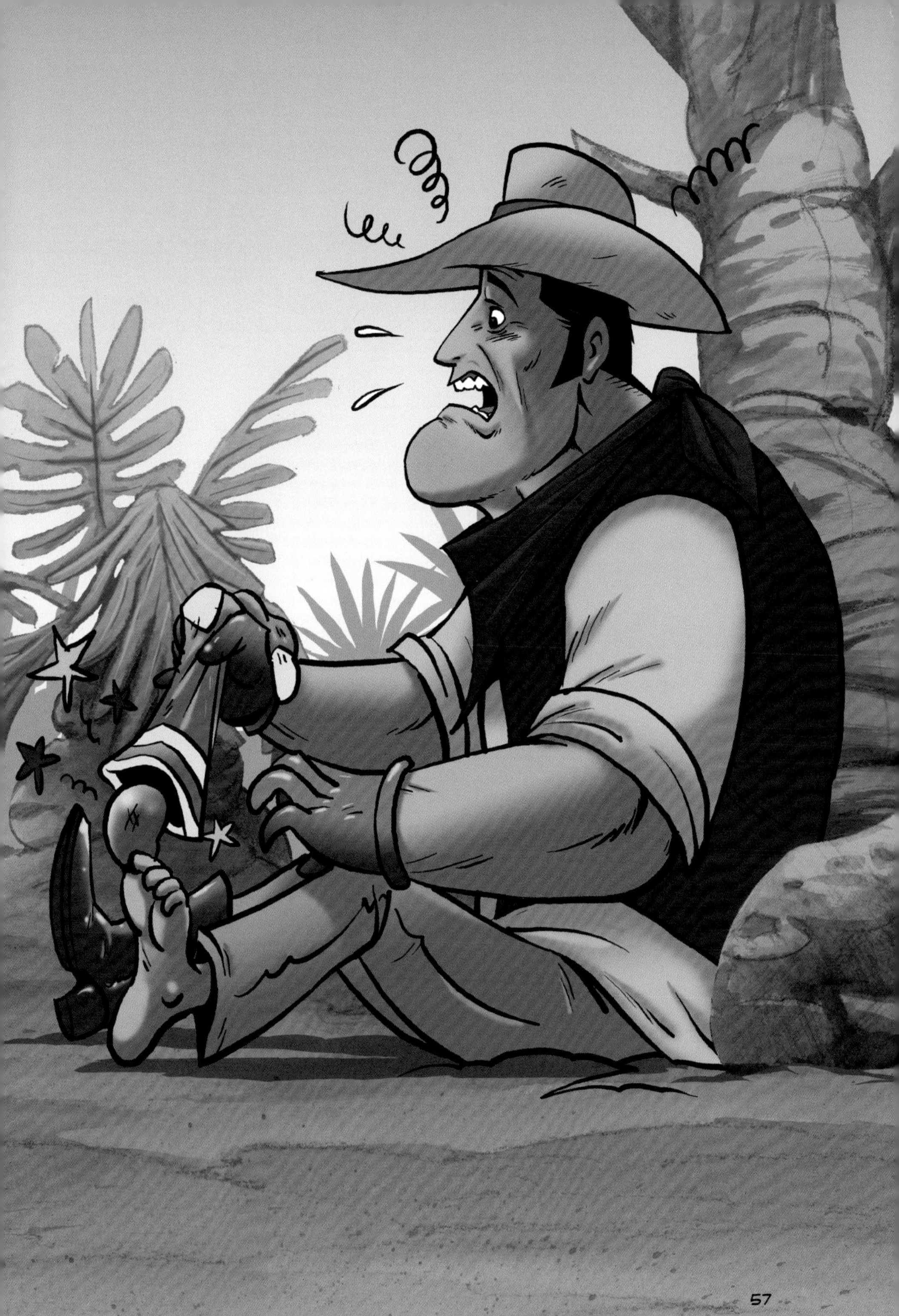

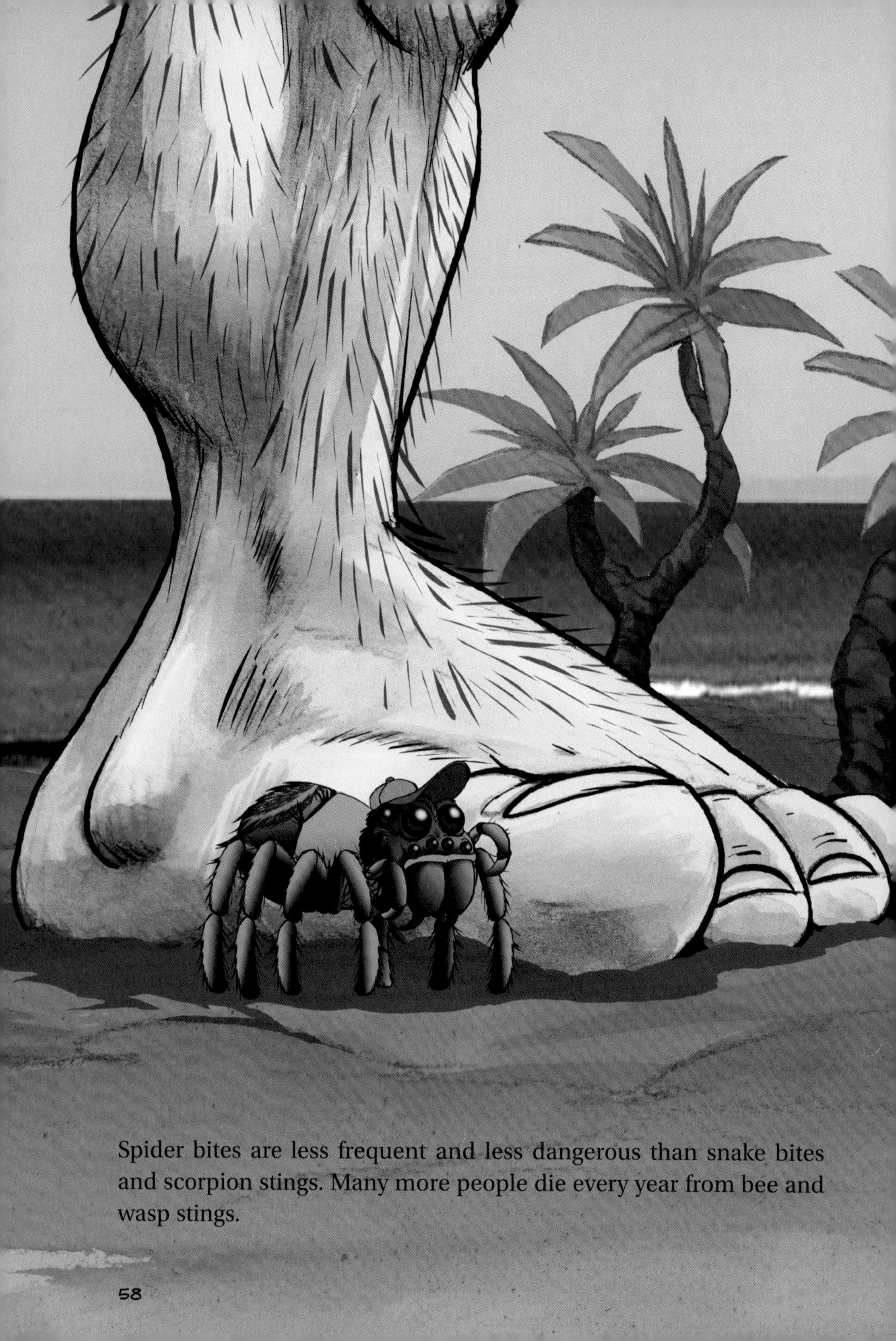

Spider bites are less frequent and less dangerous than snake bites and scorpion stings. Many more people die every year from bee and wasp stings.

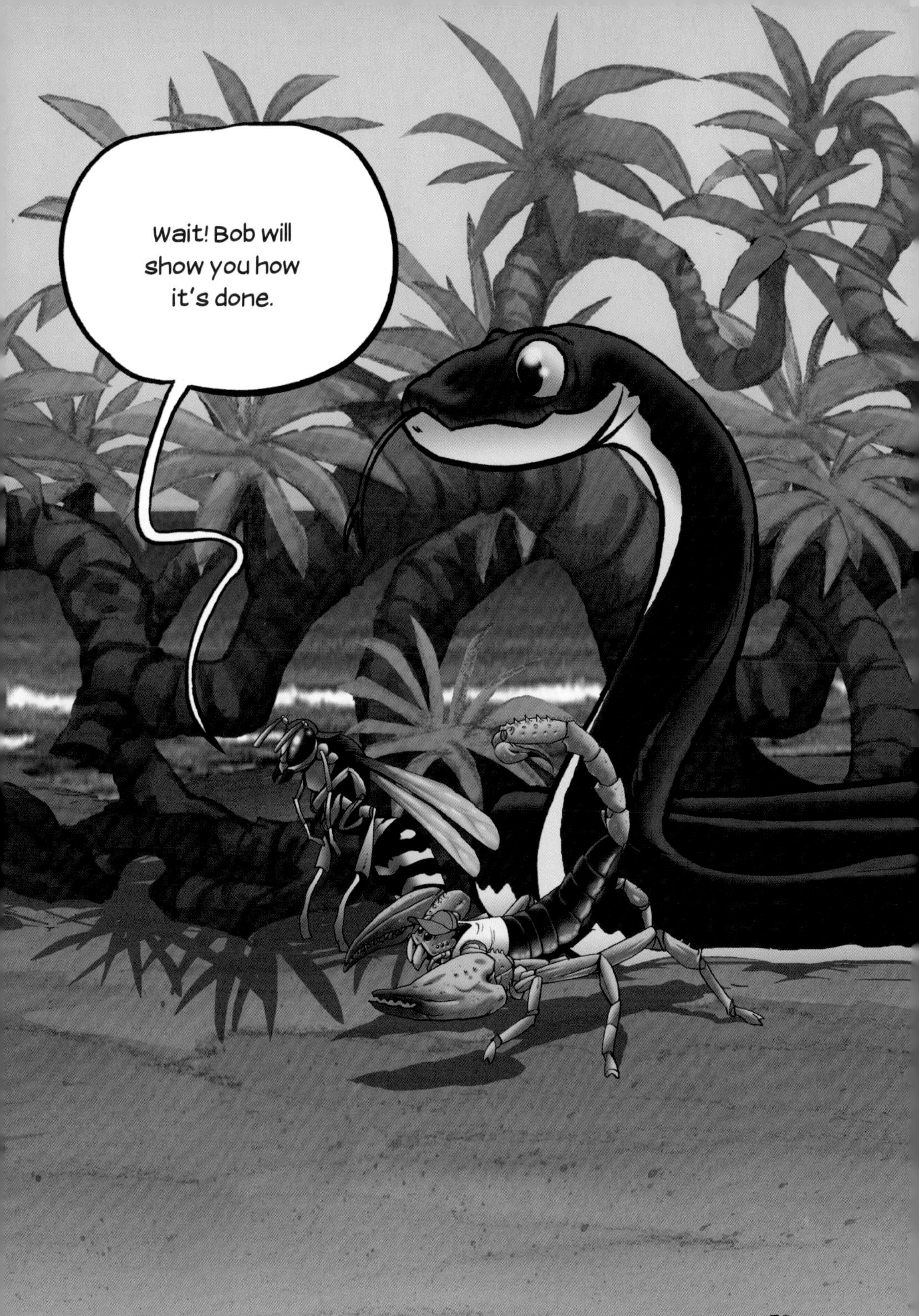
Wait! Bob will show you how it's done.

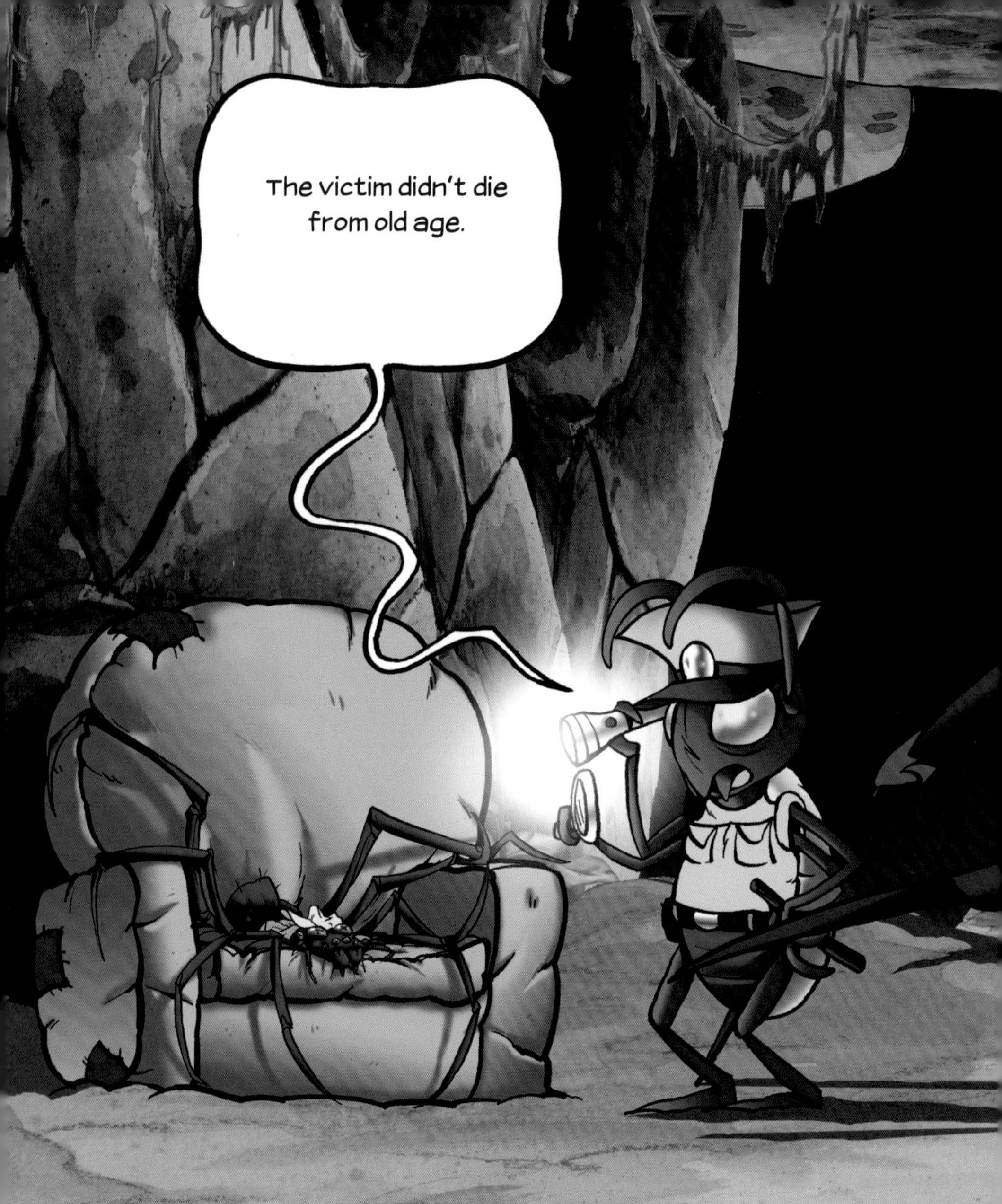
The victim didn't die from old age.

Most spiders die within a year. Females live longer than males. There are some exceptions, however. Certain tarantulas can live up to 20 years.

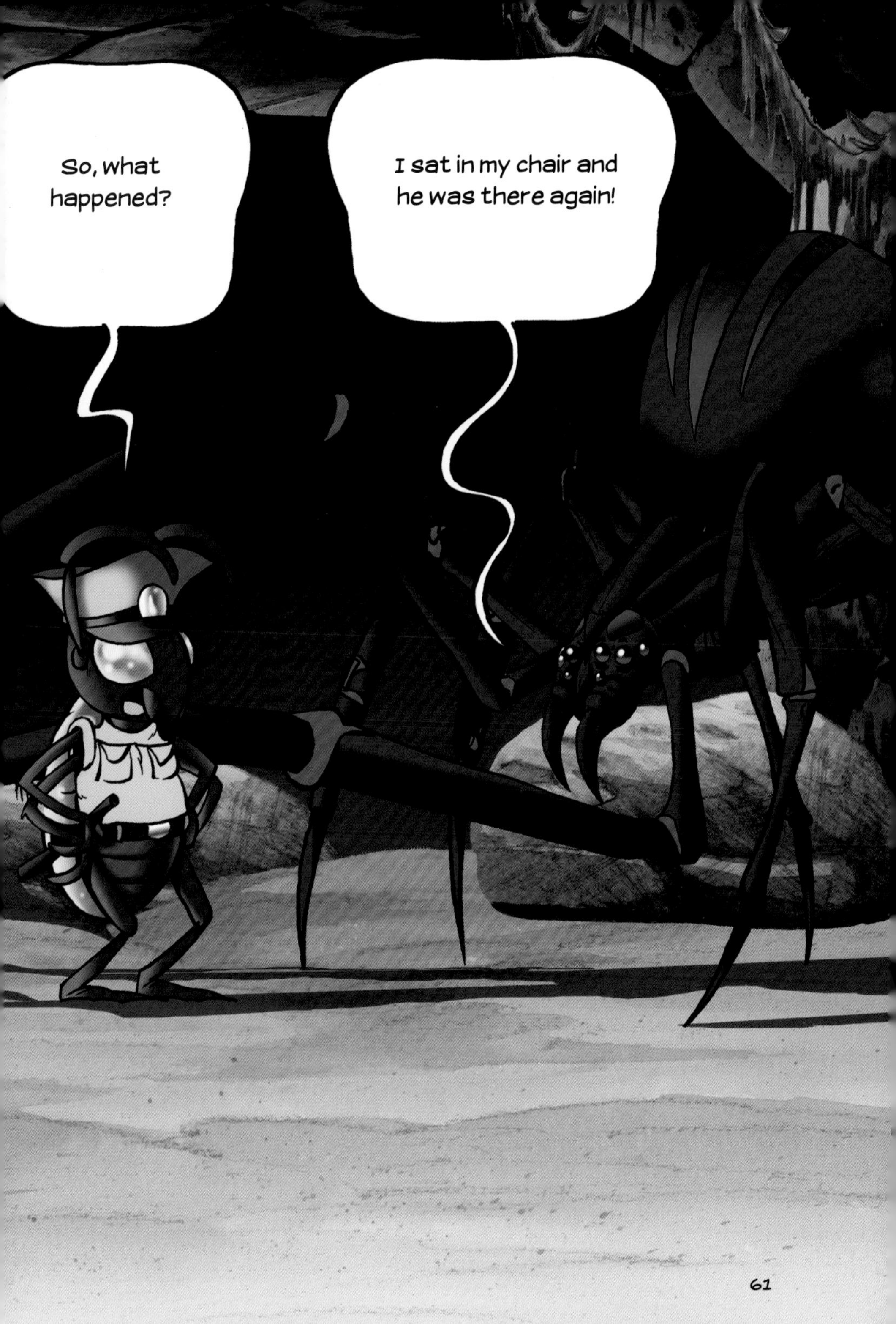
So, what happened?
I sat in my chair and he was there again!

Glossary

Carnivore a meat-eater

Climate the weather conditions of a particular area

Crustacean a group of animals, including crabs, lobsters, and shrimps

External skeleton a hard covering on the outside of an organism's body that protects and supports it

Predator a hunter that kills prey for food

Prey an organism hunted and killed by another for food

Immobilize to prevent or restrict movement

Species a classification for a group of organisms with common characteristics

Venom a poisonous secretion

Index

Other *Do You Know?* titles

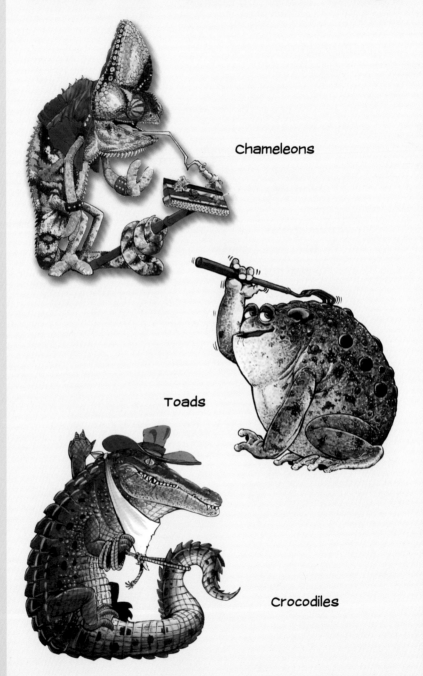

Chameleons

Toads

Crocodiles